A Blueprint
for America

William Hynson

To order additional copies of this book, contact:
Xlibris Corporation
1-888-795-4274
www.Xlibris.com
Orders@Xlibris.com
108946

TO THE AMERICAN PEOPLE

MAY OUR COUNTRY ALWAYS REMAIN STRONG AND GREAT

Table of Contents

INTRODUCTION

Look not Mournfully into the Past

It Comes not Back Again

Wisely Improve the Present

It is Thine

Go Forth to Meet the Shadowy Future

Without Fear and With a Manly Heart

Longfellow's Hyperion

These words of Longfellow have always been an inspiration to me and guided me through life. As we enter the 21st Century with a myriad of problems facing the Country it might serve all of us well if we all followed Longfellow's advice. Having been born in the depths of the Great Depression (I will be 80 years old in 2012) I have lived through a lifetime of changes. Not only changes that have taken place throughout the world but right here in the United States. Our Country has gone through wars, periods of prosperity, a major depression, numerous recessions, social changes, innovations in science and technology and perhaps most significant a tremendous increase in the population in the last 100 years growing from approximately 100 million to something in excess of 300 million which makes the United States having the world's third largest population behind China and India. Every indication shows that this population will continue to increase perhaps at an increasing rate which will bring new problems that will have to be dealt with and these problems that are the result of an increasing population may turn out to be the most significant and complex problems that our Country must deal with in the years to come.

People of every generation who reach my age have a natural tendency to look back and remember "the good old days." It is sometimes difficult to realize just how short a normal human life span is. Time goes by all too quickly and a normal human lifespan is nothing more than a brief spec in the passage of time. A human life span simply consists of all the events and happenings that occur between the time a person is born and the time they die. People can always go back in the history books and study what occurred before they were born but they will never know what is going to happen after they die. It was Adolph Hitler who once said the individual dies off but the state lives on. I think of all the people who were so active and prominent during my lifetime and who contributed so much to the progress of our Country who now lie quietly in their graves oblivious to everything that has occurred since their death. Nowhere was this emphasized more to me than when I visited the Roosevelt Estate at Hyde Park, New York and saw the grave of Franklin and Eleanor Roosevelt. When you see them resting in such a beautiful tranquil setting it is hard to realize that they were at one time at the center of the world's turbulence.

It is perhaps a destiny of life or fate that determines when a person is born and when they die. The timing is such a significant factor but one that is entirely beyond our control. I think of my father who was born in 1905. He was too young to fight in World War I and too old to fight in World War II. Had he been born five years earlier he might very well have been fighting in France during World War I. Had he been born five years later he might very well have been at Pearl Harbor in December 1941 or been at Bataan in April, 1942. A Jew born in Germany in 1850 and who died in 1930 was able to live a full life without being subjected to the horrors that would follow but if he had been born ten years later he would have become a part of those horrors. And had I been born ten years later I might very well have been fighting in the jungles of Vietnam. Timing is everything.

People my age tend to look around them and shake their heads and say the Country is going to the dogs. Changes have crept up on them which were barely noticed while they were taking place erasing and replacing everything they once fondly remembered. They find it difficult to adjust to and accept the changes that have taken place and look into the future with caution and uncertainty. To quote something Alexander Hamilton said toward the close of his life "Every day proves to me more and more that this American world was not made for me." Of course we all realize that America with all its problems is still the greatest country in the world and as the song goes once you leave New York you don't go anywhere.

One of the biggest problems that needs to be addressed is how to get the Congress and the White House to listen to and accept the will of the people. Our political system has become a victim of the special interest groups and a vastly entrenched government bureaucracy. The single individual has become a minute voice in the process of government and really has no voice at all. The best advice that I could give to anyone would be for the people to regain control over the political system. My definition of what the role of the President should be is not to attempt to implement his own personal agenda and do whatever he wants regardless of the will of the people but rather to listen to and see that the will of a majority of the people is carried out. The President should be someone who can generate ideas and solutions to problems and act as an administrator in implementing the policies that evolve from the Congress. We have seen all too often Presidents who have attempted to impose their own personal agenda against the will of a majority of the people and the Country has suffered accordingly.

This book is not intended to be a lengthy novel. Rather I have attempted to condense the main points of each issue and hit right at the heart of the various problems without going into a lot of superfluous verbiage. I thought the reader might appreciate this. Because there are so many major issues that are currently being debated and an important Presidential Election coming up in 2012 it is the purpose of this book to take each one of these issues and attempt to provide an independent and objective overview as to what the real problems are and to provide some ideas as to how they might be solved on a non-political basis. It is not the purpose of this book to attempt to influence public opinion in any manner. The American people have every right and in fact have an obligation to think for themselves and to make their own decisions on the issues facing the Country without being influenced by any political force. But my hope is that this will give the American people some ideas to think about and contemplate when they make their decisions.

Every issue debated in the Congress is subjected to Democratic views and Republican views each heavily influenced by the lobbyists and the special interests. This is where the problem lies. There must be a way to eliminate politics and special interests when discussing these issues and to simply look for the right solution. There should be no such thing as a Democratic solution or a Republican solution. The only solution must be the correct solution. The problems are complex and are going to require input from many different sources if we are ever going to come up with the right solutions and put the United States on the right course. Unfortunately, politics will always come into play in debating these issues and the resulting solutions are not always in the best interest of the American people.

The single one most important issue facing the American people today is the direction the Country will take. That is will the people vote to go in the direction of big government, excessive spending, higher taxes and potential financial collapse all leading to socialism with all its ominous consequences or will they vote to maintain democracy and the free enterprise system, to bring spending under control, create prosperity for the American people and keep government off the backs of the people? The direction the Country will take and the form of government it will have is the most important issue facing the American people and it should transcend all other issues. When the American people go into the voting booth the only issue that they should be concerned with is whether the Country is going to preserve democracy and individual opportunity and freedom and reduce the role of government or whether it is going to head into socialism with all its ominous consequences and total government control over the people.

The path we have been traveling down is one that will lead directly to socialism as the role of government has become larger and larger over the years. Unfortunately, this cannot be attributable to any one individual. If it were that simple it would be relatively easy to just vote that individual out of office. We have not yet reached the point where a dictator stands ready to step in and assume total control over the people. Rather this path to socialism has been created by government simply feeding on itself year after year and getting bigger and bigger in the process. The American people have created a monster they no longer have any control over and which has the potential of consuming them all. When people say that the size of government should be reduced that reduction should refer to the power and control government exercises over the people and not merely the physical size of government in terms of personnel and spending. Of course the number of government employees and the amount of money government spends is a direct indication of the power and control government exercises over the people. In spite of the large number of politicians who have run for office over the years promising to reduce the size of government they have had little success as government continues to grow and expand its power and control over the people and right now in 2011 the potential to continue this growth is greater than ever. Once socialism becomes firmly established fascism will not be far behind. I would like to quote a few lines from John Gunther's book "Inside USA" which was published in 1947:

> "Fascism will come in disguised as socialism. A man will make every promise to the under-possessed, and undeniably improve their circumstances; he will appeal to almost every shade of liberal; on the horizon, emerging he will seem to be a savior, a disinterested messiah. The awakening comes later—with abrogation of civil liberties, military rule, seizure of the electorate, building of a Hitler-like machine, selling out to the big interests who were originally the opposition, concentration camps for the first followers and all the dissidents, and in the end bilking the people of what they thought they had."

We can only hope this will never happen in America.

TOPIC I

JOB CREATION

With all the concern over job losses and unemployment it may be time to rethink the entire issue from a different perspective. The so-called unemployment rate which is currently around 9.2% has become a meaningless and obsolete statistic. It simply does not give a true insight into what the real problems are. What good is a statistic that eliminates those who have simply dropped out of the labor force? If a million people suddenly just gave up all hope of finding a job and quit looking everyone would cheer since it would mean an improvement in the unemployment rate. This does not make any sense and the people who just drop out may have a more serious problem than those who continue looking for work. What must be determined is just how serious the unemployment problem is in the United States and whether there can be permanent prosperity while carrying a large unemployment load. There are three factors that will keep unemployment at a high level probably for years to come and possibly permanently.

The first has to do with the demographics of the United States. The total population is currently around 310 million and growing year by year. Ten years from now the population could be around 340 million.

13

Is it reasonable to think that enough jobs can be created to absorb this increase in the population? If we cannot create enough jobs when the population is 310 million how are we going to handle the increase in the population? I shudder to think what will happen when the Country's population reaches 400 or 500 million or more 50 or 100 years from now. While jobs will be created the population is growing at a faster rate which will keep unemployment at a high level. The 15 million or so currently unemployed represent approximately 5% of the total population. In many respects to say that only 5% of a total population of 300 million are unemployed actually seems like a reasonably low figure. It is hard to see it going much lower.

With a population in the 300 to 350 million range what needs to be figured out is just how many people should be working to support this population. It is logical to assume that as the population increases the workforce needed to support it does not need to increase at the same rate. When people say that we need to create more jobs the first thing that goes through my mind is just what do they mean by a job? How do they define it? There are jobs and there are jobs. Are they talking about high paying jobs or low paying jobs? Are they talking about jobs with substantial benefits or jobs with minimum or no benefits? What is a reasonable wage? If someone loses their $50,000 a year job and takes a job that pays $25,000 a year it has no effect on the unemployment statistics since a job has been lost and a job has been gained. But it represents a tremendous economic loss to the individual. Further, when people talk about the need to create jobs are they talking about jobs that are on a career path and have a future or are they simply talking about going to work every day in a dead end job with no future? Is a job merely something to provide a paycheck or is it something that will provide personal satisfaction and fulfillment? It is an oversimplification for people to talk about jobs in a general sense without getting into the specifics as to what types of jobs they are talking about.

The important factor that should be closely examined is not the number of people who are working or the number of people who are unemployed but rather the number of people who are working and the wages they earn. It is this total earnings amount that determines the prosperity level. Let us assume 150 million people have jobs and the average wage is $40,000 a year. This amounts to six trillion dollars of earnings. Now if 50 million jobs are lost but the remaining 100 million people earn an average of $60,000 a year it still amounts to six trillion dollars. In other words it is possible to have fewer people employed but earning more and still have the same impact on the economy. Therefore the most important factor becomes the wages earned and the question then becomes is it better to have more jobs paying lower wages or fewer jobs paying higher wages if the economic impact is the same?

It would almost seem that the solution to the unemployment problem may not be to attempt to create more jobs which is going to be very difficult but rather to find a way to put adequate purchasing power into the hands of every individual since spending is the engine that will drive the economy to prosperity. As we look to the future the unemployment problem will only get worse. Not only will the actual number of unemployed increase along with the increase in the population but also it should be noted that if on average the wages being paid on the newly created jobs are less than the wages for the jobs that have been eliminated this in itself will lower the standard of living for all Americans.

The second factor that will keep unemployment at a high level is the global economy. It is probable that we would have entered into a global economy sooner or later as there are a number of benefits there from but what has never been clearly explained to the American people is that in a global economy the wealth of a country and its jobs are going to flow out of those countries with high labor costs and go into those countries with low labor costs. There is a leveling process that will over time reduce the standard of living for those living in high labor cost countries and raise the standard of living for those living in low labor cost countries. As long as there are millions of workers in countries around the world who are willing to work for wages far less than what the American worker needs jobs will be going to those countries. The biggest problem the United States faces is that there is a large gap between what the average worker needs in the way of income to enjoy the "American" way of life and what an employer can afford to pay to be both profitable and competitive in the global economy. The global economy is not going to subsidize the American worker in order to provide him with a standard of living far higher than that in other countries. There is one way that the United Sates can benefit in a global economy and that is by manufacturing products of such high quality that they cannot be duplicated elsewhere in the world thereby creating a world wide demand for them and also by creating products that no other country in the world is capable of producing.

The average middle class American family probably has mortgage or rent payments of approximately $1,500 a month, car loan payments of around $500 a month and substantial credit card payments. Assume that this family needs $25,000 to $30,000 a year just to pay these monthly debts. Add another $25,000 to $30,000 a year for food, clothing, utilities, automobile expenses, personal expenses and other miscellaneous expenses. This includes providing each family member with a computer, cell phone and wide screen TV set all of which have become necessities and which are expensive in themselves. We are now up to $50,000 to $60,000 a year and this is before medical expenses, college tuition payments and retirement savings. And this does not begin to include any amounts spent on vacations or luxury items or for money put aside for a rainy day fund. Add to this an amount for income and social security taxes and you are looking at around $100,000 a year. But this does not include employer expenses such as matching social security payments, insurance premiums and other employee expenses. Now the total is around $120,000 a year which translated to a 40 hour work week comes out to around $60 an hour. It is no wonder so many jobs have been sent overseas where the labor costs are probably half this amount. Large corporations cannot afford to pay this and remain profitable and competitive. Many people say that small businesses are the key to reducing unemployment but small businesses cannot afford to hire people at $60 a hour and most owners probably do not make this much themselves. Joe the plumber cannot afford to hire an assistant at this wage rate. The real challenge is to find a way to fill the gap between what the employee needs and what the business can afford to pay.

Government bail out programs and subsidies are not the answer particularly when funds are handed out with no strings attached. Lowering taxes on business is not the answer since this does not address the problem of high labor costs. What needs to be done is for the Federal Government and the various state governments to get together and jointly provide funds to selected businesses that will directly reduce their labor costs. These funds should be looked upon as an investment that will be returned with interest and will not in any way be considered a misuse of taxpayer funds. For example, a company with labor costs of two million dollars would show that as an expense which would reduce its net income. If this company received a payment of one million dollars towards its labor costs it would then show on its expense statement labor costs of two million dollars less a payment received of one million dollars and net labor costs of one million dollars thereby increasing net income by one million dollars. Unlike receiving tax relief this would actually enable the company to pay more in taxes since it would show an increase in net income and it would also be an incentive to hire more employees since the company would be making more money. At the same time it would be able to pay its employees the higher wages necessary to support their lifestyle which would put more dollars into the economy thereby increasing overall prosperity.

The third factor keeping unemployment at a high level is the objective of many businesses to resort to labor savings devices and to rely on increased productivity from their existing employees. By reducing labor costs a company reduces its expenses which increases profits. But increasing profits by reducing labor costs is not the same as increasing profits by selling more product. In the long run it will have a counter productive effect on the economy. This is why the idea of having payments made to a company to directly reduce labor costs is the only answer. Had this sort of program been in effect all along it is doubtful that so many jobs would have been sent overseas. Instead of losing jobs more jobs would have been created. Instead of a shrinking economy the economy would have expanded. More people would have been employed, more people would be spending, more businesses would be making money and more taxes would be collected thus solving many of the state and local budget problems that currently exist.

Sometimes the answer is in full view but goes unnoticed. The concept of lowering labor costs to the point where businesses will hire more people makes all the sense in the world. The best thing about this approach is that companies will hire more people, they will make more money and pay more taxes, they will be more competitive in the global economy and the employees will benefit from the higher wages and be able to spend more thus providing a strong engine to keep the economy going at a high level. And the investment that the Federal Government and the states make would be repaid with interest as there would be a rippling effect throughout the economy which would generate additional tax revenues. We might even begin to see the "Made in USA" label once again.

Everyone knows the history of the textile industry in the United States which was at one time a thriving industry in New England employing thousands of workers. It is difficult for anyone to imagine today while driving through some of the old factory towns and seeing the huge abandoned buildings the thousands of workers who at one time were employed there. What happened was a case where wages simply got too high and the industry decided they could save money by moving to the south were labor was far less costly. Much of this movement took place in the 1940s and 1950s which left the factory towns in New England looking like ghost towns. Beginning 10 or 15 years ago the textile industry again moved this time out of the United States. Workers in Central America and the Far East could be employed at a substantial savings in labor costs. As was the case with the New England towns this had a devastating effect on many of the southern towns where the textile factories had been located.

I have often thought abut the textile industry in my home state of North Carolina which in the last 10 or15 years or so has probably shed around 100,000 jobs due to moving their operations out of the United States. Using an average wage of $40,000 a year this amounts to four billion dollars of earnings each year that is not being spent in North Carolina. If we assume that the textile industry is saving half that amount by using foreign labor we are looking at savings of two billion dollars a year in labor costs for the textile industry. What would have been wrong if the Federal Government and the State of North Carolina had got together and told the textile industry that they would jointly pay the two billion dollars a year to keep the textile industry in North Carolina thereby removing the financial incentive for the textile industry to move out of the Country? Right upfront there would be about two billion dollars of savings from not having to pay unemployment compensation. Instead of 100,000 textile workers unemployed there would now be 100,000 workers employed spending their four billion dollars of wages in the local economies thereby generating hundreds of millions of dollars in sales taxes. There would be hundreds of millions of dollars paid in federal and state income taxes. And the textile industry itself would be paying more taxes since it would be showing an increase in net income. All of this tax revenue would be recovered from the first round of spending and as the dollars were recycled throughout the economy there would be additional tax revenues from each additional spending cycle. There would also be additional hiring as businesses would need more help to handle the increased economic activity thereby reducing unemployment even more. This in turn would generate additional tax revenues. The bottom line is that the investment that the Federal and State governments would be making in labor costs would generate a tremendous increase in economic activity and they would recover much and probably more of their investment from the increased income and sales taxes that would be generated.

Another example of how high labor costs can cost America business has to do with the automobile industry. Probably not many people today remember the Union settlement with the Ford Motor Company back in the late 1940s. In those days the CIO, which later merged with the American Federation of Labor and became the AFL-CIO, represented the auto workers and always started negotiations for a new contract with the Ford Motor Company. Of the other two of the big three auto makers General Motors was considered too big and powerful for the Union to begin negotiations with and Chrysler was considered too small and not influential enough. The thinking was that if the Union could reach an agreement with Ford the other companies would go along. The settlement that was reached made headlines and shocked many people because of the generous benefits the Union was able to extract. It was considered to be a highly favorable settlement for the Union. What this did was to cause the automobile industry to increase the prices on their cars in order to pay the higher labor costs resulting from the settlement. At the same time the Japanese economy was recovering from World War II. Japan had two things in its favor an abundance of cheap hardworking industrious labor and the technical knowledge to make a superior car. As everyone knows the result of this was that the Japanese were able to make substantial inroads into the world automobile market and succeeded in taking a large share away from the United States auto makers. Again high labor costs diverted business out of the United States.

In the last ten years or so we have seen the United States go from the wealthiest and most highly industrialized country in the world to a country on the verge of bankruptcy. Not only has the Federal Government reached this point but states, municipalities and private citizens are all over their heads in debt. The situation is serious. Just look at the mortgage foreclosures alone and the depressed real estate market. The United States and China have completely reversed their roles in the world economy. China is now the worlds banker and industrial leader and very few items are purchased in the United States that do not have a made in China label on them. This all began with high labor costs in the United States and low labor costs in China. And because there are other countries such as Brazil and India that are rapidly developing their economies it is possible that there will be a further erosion in the financial and economic power of the United States as well as a continued decrease in the overall standard of living. It is absolutely essential that the United States find a way to keep its workers in the United States and to regain business that has been lost to foreign countries.

The national debt of the United States is currently approximately 14 trillion dollars. It has become a serious problem that has the potential of forcing the United States into bankruptcy. There is now a fierce battle going on between the Democratic Party and the Republican Party over spending which has grown out of control. Of course there are two things that could be done to prevent an actual default on the debt but neither would have a positive impact on the economy. One would be to raise everyone's taxes to an astronomical level in effect wiping out life long savings for many individuals. The other would be to simply print as much money as needed and flood the country with worthless dollars again virtually wiping out everyone's savings. At the end of World War II the United States was faced with a huge debt resulting from financing the war. We were able to pay down that debt and enter into a period of prosperity because at the end of the war the United States was the only major country in the world whose industry had not been destroyed by the war. We now no longer have that luxury as we have lost our position as the world's industrial leader to China and China has become the world's banker.

To say the United States is currently undergoing an economic malaise may be understating the situation somewhat. But the economy is stagnant and not growing. People face uncertainty and lack the confidence to invest in the future. What we need are enlightened government policies that will provide business with the confidence to want to expand and hire more employees. The alternative is to simply continue down the path of self-destruction.

The best way to place the economy on a sound footing and reduce unemployment is to insure that every American has adequate purchasing power and this not only means the wealthy but more importantly it means the middle and lower income classes. Spending is the engine that will drive the economy ahead and the only way to do this is to let people keep more of what they earn. The failure to create jobs, the impact of higher prices and the overall uncertainty as to which direction the Country will take will more likely push the Country into a depression rather than bring increased prosperity. I have mentioned that one way to improve the economy and reduce unemployment is by having the Federal Government and the various states jointly make payments to selected businesses that will directly reduce their labor costs so that they will hire more people. There is another solution that I would recommend and that is to greatly reduce income tax rates. I propose giving every taxpayer a $100,000 exemption and taxing incomes above $100,000 at a maximum of 20%. This would be a straight 20% based on total income earned and there would be no itemized deductions allowed. It is time the tax code is simplified. If a middle income taxpayer owes $3,000 in income taxes let him keep that entire amount which he can then spend. The 800 billion dollar stimulus package did not improve the economy. It was a complete waste of taxpayer dollars. It would have been far better if that 800 billion dollars had been distributed directly to the taxpayers so that they could have increased their spending. Had this been done we might very well be out of the recession and there would have been a large drop in unemployment. But this is all hindsight. It would also be hoped that the states that have income taxes would adopt a comparable reduction in their tax rates.

We need to re-examine how the Federal Government is financed. An income tax simply removes purchasing power from every taxpayer since they have less to spend. It is not the total answer. It is also not fair to increase income taxes on those who have been able through their hard work and individual initiative to substantially increase their income. Rather than penalize success we need to provide opportunities and incentives for those with low incomes to improve their lot. Redistribution of the wealth is not the answer. The answer lies in creating a climate in which everyone will have the opportunity to create their own wealth. In fact, in many countries that have attempted a policy of redistributing the wealth it is not unreasonable to assume that those who were supposed to be benefiting actually found that they ended up being worse off than they were before. What I would like to see is a greater reliance on taxes based on spending as opposed to taxes based on income. In fact I would like to see all state and local sales taxes abolished and replaced by one national sales tax of say 12% on every dollar that is spent with certain items such as food and healthcare costs being exempted. This 12 % would be divided 8% to the individual states and 4% to the Federal Government. Thus, the Federal Government would be supported in part by both the tax on spending and the income tax on incomes of $100,000 and over.

Since there are so many people who want to quickly oppose the idea of a tax on spending because they feel it shifts the tax burden from the wealthy to the lower income groups I am going to clarify my tax proposal. The fact is that my plan does just the opposite. The higher the income the more tax that will be paid. On the income side I propose exempting all income up to $100,000 from being taxed. For incomes from $100,000 up to $249,999 the tax would be 5%. For incomes from $250,000 up to $499,999 the tax would be 10%. For incomes from $500,000 up to $999,999 the tax would be 15% and for incomes of $1,000,000 and over the tax would be 20%. Under this plan there would be no itemized deductions and the tax would be paid on total income.

As for the tax on spending I am proposing the exemption of all expenses that fall into the category of basic living expenses. These would include, food, utilities, mortgage and rent payments, healthcare costs and other similar necessary living expenses. These expenses normally take the first $50,000 or so of a person's income so anyone making less than this amount would not pay any tax at all either on income or on spending. The tax on spending would only kick in after these basic expenses have been paid and would only be paid on the discretionary income that would be left over after these basic expenses. It is primarily designed to cover the large ticket and luxury items that only those with discretionary spending power would be able to purchase anyway. The higher the income the more discretionary income there is and the more that would be paid in taxes. This is actually a very fair and reasonable tax system. The whole concept revolves around the lowering of taxes on income in order to put more purchasing power into the hands of all taxpayers. When tax dollars are taken away from people up front they have no opportunity to spend that money. By shifting the tax to the spending side people will at least have a choice of whether or not to spend the extra dollars they have. The fact that a substantial amount of these dollars will be spent will be a direct positive stimulus on the economy and the increased tax revenue from the improving economy will more than offset the lower taxes that individuals will be paying.

The United States is probably the only country in the world that simply looks the other way when people enter the country illegally. I know of no country that would allow an American citizen to just walk in and demand a job, healthcare benefits and education for their children not that any American citizen would want to anyway. I suggest to the millions of illegal immigrants currently in the United States that what the American people are looking for is a sense of fairness. Those Americans who are law abiding citizens have difficulty accepting the fact that so many people now in our Country illegally are receiving the types of benefits that most American citizens have had to work so hard for.

This situation reminds me of the days when I was living in Connecticut and on Sundays during the summer we would drive over to the Rhode Island beaches. As we got closer to the beach the traffic would begin to back up and there would be a long line of cars bumper to bumper just crawling along. While we were inching our way towards the beach there would always be a few cars that from way in the back would drive out along the shoulder of the road and pass all the cars that had been patiently waiting in front of them and then cut in up in front of the line of cars. To my knowledge no one ever stopped them and they were in effect rewarded for doing something illegal.

But let us get one thing clear. The American people have nothing against any Hispanics. The American people are a very open and fair minded people. They recognize the potential value and contributions that these immigrants can make to our Society. It is not because these people are Hispanic that creates the problem. It is because they have entered the country illegally and this would apply to people of any nationality. I know that if I were a decent law abiding Hispanic American citizen I would be highly resentful of any politician who attempted to win my vote by offering benefits to people who entered the country illegally.

I believe that if given a chance these illegal immigrants will indeed take full advantage of the opportunities afforded them and become like the legal immigrants before them hardworking and useful citizens and who will become part of the melting pot that made America great. The first hurdle should be to resolve the illegality question which should be fairly easy to do. Once that is resolved I am certain that these immigrants would be welcomed with open arms.

I fully agree with those individuals who talk about how much immigrants have meant to this Country in the past and how much they have contributed to our Country's success. We are all descended from immigrants if we were to go back far enough. The main distinction is that our ancestors were legal immigrants who entered the United States through a legal process and proudly became part of the melting pot that made our Country great. These legal immigrants assimilated into the American culture, learned the English language and became hardworking, law abiding citizens.

As for the relationship of illegal immigrants to our Country's current unemployment problem an argument can be made that the illegal immigrants for the most part fill the low paying menial types of jobs that no American worker wants to fill. We do not seem to have reached the point where the unemployed in the United States have become so desperate that they are lining up to fill these jobs. In this regard there is a vast difference in the mentality of the American worker today as compared with the American workers during the Great Depression. In those days workers who lost their jobs had no sense of pride. They simply went out and did whatever they could do to make a few dollars. They took jobs as dishwashers and stood on street corners selling apples. It is hard to imagine today people reducing themselves to this level. At least I have not seen anyone standing on street corners selling apples. We are now living in a more status conscious image conscious society and no one wants to do something that they feel is beneath their dignity. This, of course, provides an opportunity for the illegal immigrants as they are willing to fill the very types of jobs that no American worker is willing to perform. However useful the illegal immigrants are in doing this sort of work it does not erase the fact that they have entered the United States illegally. What do you suppose would happen if twelve million unemployed Americans crossed the border into Mexico or Canada and demanded healthcare benefits and education for their children? We have to be realistic about this. When something is illegal it is illegal until such time as the law is changed. We simply cannot allow people to flout our laws and live as if they have done nothing wrong.

Now we will never go out and round up 11 or 12 million illegal immigrants and deport them back to their country of origin. In many countries around the world this is exactly what would be done. But the United States has always been a humanitarian nation where we place a high value on human rights. Recognizing that these illegal immigrants have much to offer we need to take steps to resolve the problem once and for all and to put an end to the debate over what should be done with these people. They should be given every opportunity to become useful citizens who will contribute to the betterment of our Country's future and improve their own future in the process. To accomplish this the following steps should be taken:

1. Every illegal immigrant should be required to register with a local authority. This information should go into a national data bank so that people with criminal backgrounds and potential terrorist threats can be detected. This is actually for the benefit of and the protection of all illegal immigrants.

2. A photo identification should be required for every illegal immigrant. I would add that a photo identification should be required of everyone including American citizens when they show up to vote. I myself would be proud to comply with this. It is one way of eliminating voting fraud.

3. Every illegal immigrant should have a sponsor or employer who will assume responsibility for the illegal immigrant. The sponsor or employer will pay the sum of $1,000 a year for three years to the locality where the illegal immigrant resides. This is partly to serve as a fine for illegally entering the United States and partly to reimburse the locality for tax dollars used to support the illegal immigrant.

4. If an illegal immigrant remains gainfully employed for a period of three years and if they have no criminal record and if they take a course in the English language and a course in American History they will be eligible to become an American citizen.

5. Children born to an illegal immigrant during the first three years will be considered citizens of the mother's country of origin. If at the end of three years the mother becomes an American citizen any children born during the previous three years will automatically become American citizens.

These are just a few ideas on how we might deal with the problem of illegal immigrants and are not necessarily the final solution. I suggest them as a starting point in finding a solution to the problem. I am certain that those illegal immigrants who are allowed to remain in the United States and who abide by our laws and become good citizens will like their legal predecessors before them turn out to be productive and useful citizens who can make an important contribution to the future success of the United States.

TOPIC II

HEALTHCARE

I can remember way back in 1950 when I was living in New York State a family friend mentioning that their company had just started a new benefit for the employees called Blue Cross Insurance. It was supposed to help pay doctor and hospital expenses and everyone thought it was a great idea. Little by little more companies began to offer this type of insurance to their employees but something unforeseen happened in the process. As more and more people began to have their health costs covered by insurance health costs began going up. In those days our family physician charged $3.00 for an office visit and $5.00 for a house call. Believe it or not our family physician was still making house calls. A room at the local hospital was around $25.00 a night. The big increases in health costs came after the enactment of Medicare in the 1960s. It was as if the healthcare providers saw this insurance coverage as a large anonymous pot of gold they could just dip their hands into and they could simply tell their patients not to worry about the higher costs because the insurance company was going to be paying.

When Medicare was first created it seemed like a good thing to many senior citizens and over the years it has undoubtedly been beneficial to millions of senior citizens. Of course, we will never know what might have happened to these people if Medicare had never been enacted in the first place and whether these millions of senior citizens would have been better off or worse off. Certainly someone would have stepped in and filled the gap had Medicare never been enacted. Today Medicare has become an entrenched household word in every senior citizen household. It is as much a part of the daily life of every senior citizen as apple pie and motherhood. Unfortunately, most senior citizens do not focus on the financial aspects of Medicare and see that it is a sinking ship. They simply take it for granted and expect it to be around forever. The 500 billion dollar reduction in Medicare benefits to finance the recently enacted healthcare legislation did not seem to arouse much reaction from the senior citizens. Nor has the potential increase in the Medicare Part B premium caused much alarm. Perhaps if for the first time the senior citizens see an actual reduction in the amount of their social security check they will wake up to the fact that Medicare is in serious trouble. The senior citizens have gone two years without a cost of living increase and we can only hope that there will be some relief soon.

Those who suggest that the senior citizens are better off with Medicare conveniently fail to emphasize that further reductions in benefits and increases in premiums will become a way of life if Medicare continues in its present form. Most importantly they fail to point out that as Medicare reimbursements to doctors are reduced more and more doctors across the United States will no longer accept Medicare patients leaving the senior citizens without access to any healthcare. Suggesting that the senior citizens are better off with Medicare is tantamount to telling the passengers on the Titanic that they should remain on board. It would appear that the real motive behind the effort to keep Medicare is mostly political and that increasing the power and control of government over the people and the health care system is the real reason since it must be obvious that

Medicare will become increasingly less beneficial to the senior citizens as time goes on.

Regardless of what Medicare has accomplished in the past it has now become a vast government bureaucracy. No one knows how many millions of dollars are paid out in fraudulent claims each year. I know from a personal incident involving my wife that this is a serious problem. About a year ago or so she received the usual Medicare summary indicating how much Medicare paid on a particular claim. In this instance Medicare indicated they paid a claim to a doctor my wife had never heard of and showing the medical group the doctor belonged to. I was unable to track down the medical group on the internet but managed to find the doctor's name. It turned out that the doctor was with a different medical group. When I called up that group I was told that they had been having problems with a fraudulent medical group that was using their doctors in order to put in Medicare claims. I then called Medicare and asked them how they could pay a claim to a fraudulent medical group that apparently did not exist. The answer I got was that they cannot possibly check out every claim and accordingly routinely pay these claims. I suspect that these sorts of problems will only increase over time and have concluded that it is time to break up Medicare as it now exists simply because it has become too big and unwieldy. There is no doubt in my mind that the private sector could provide far more beneficial and less costly health care benefits.

What I am proposing is the creation of six regional private (non government) health providers. This would include the Northeast, Mid Atlantic, Southeast, Midwest, Southwest and the Pacific Northwest areas. They would be non-profit organizations that is there would be no stockholders looking for dividends. They should be set up on a cooperative basis with the senior citizens who are the beneficiaries being the owners. The senior citizens would have voting rights and could vote on management and policy matters. In the event there was a profit at the end of a fiscal year it would be returned to the senior citizens in the form of a premium reduction. This would have the effect of splitting up Medicare into six regional groups which being smaller would be able to operate more efficiently than Medicare which has become so large and unwieldy. The following would apply to each of these regional cooperative health providers:

1. There would be an automatic transfer from Medicare to the health provider covering the area where the senior citizen is located. The senior citizen would not have to do anything. It would be no different than having a bank account in one bank and finding out that the bank was being acquired by a larger bank. Material would be sent to the senior citizen describing how the system would work. For the most part the senior citizen would not notice anything different;

2. Every doctor, hospital and medical provider would be required to accept this insurance. There would never be an instance where a patient would go to a doctor and be told the doctor does not accept the patient's insurance;

3. These health providers would be set up similar to the Medicare advantage plans whereby they would provide coverage for doctor visits, hospitalization, medical supplies, prescription drug coverage and vision and dental coverage. It would not be necessary to carry any supplemental healthcare insurance;

4. Under this healthcare system the senior citizens would never receive a bill. There would be no deductibles, no co-payments and no annual or lifetime maximum limit on benefits. When a patient goes to a doctor the doctor will send the bill to the health provider. The two parties will then negotiate a fair and reasonable amount and that will be the final amount paid. The patient will

never be involved in the billing process. By leaving the patient out of the billing process the dollar savings in bookkeeping and paper work will amount to millions. Depending on how the numbers work out it is possible that some variation of this Section may be appropriate. For example, if a patient's visits to doctors exceed a certain number during a calendar year or if the number of days spent in a hospital exceed a certain number a co-payment might be required for the times this number is exceeded. This would mean that someone who incurs excessive healthcare costs might end up paying somewhat more than someone whose yearly costs are at a minimum. Obviously this sort of provision requires a lot of thought in order to get it right;

5. The premiums would be shared by the Federal Government and the individual senior citizen. This is only right since the money in the Medicare trust fund has already been provided by the senior citizens through their payroll deductions and represents their own money. A substantial portion of these funds should be set aside for a catastrophic emergency fund to help with cases where someone incurs substantial costs over and above what the health provider should reasonably be expected to cover. The objective should be to finance the overall costs of healthcare in a manner that will result in a lower cost to government and a lower cost to the average senior citizen but at the same time provide greater benefits. One possible alternative might be to establish a sliding scale formula whereby the premiums are based on the income level of each individual senior citizen;

6. A regulatory body would be established in order to control premium increases and to serve in an ombudsman role to resolve any disputes.

If properly presented to the senior citizens I am certain that this plan would gain widespread acceptance. There has been one plan proposed whereby vouchers would be given out to senior citizens who could then choose a healthcare plan other than Medicare. The proposal does not affect current senior citizens but would take effect sometime in the future. Unfortunately, this proposal met with strong rejection by a majority of the senior citizens who are afraid of losing their Medicare. The problem is that this proposal was thrust upon the senior citizens suddenly without any significant groundwork being laid and the opposition was quick to jump in and frighten the senior citizens into thinking that they would be worse off than they currently are with Medicare. What needs to be done is to launch a through educational program directed to the senior citizens explaining in detail the serious financial position Medicare is currently in. I think there are so many pluses in my plan that once it is fully explained the senior citizens will realize that it is a far better option for them.

One possibility might be for these regional cooperative health providers to provide coverage to anyone regardless of age. Is it really necessary to have a separate healthcare program just for people over age 65? I see no reason why everyone should not have the same health benefits and be covered by the same type of insurance plan. While this idea might have some merits it could possibly run into resistance from the for profit health plans currently in existence where the patients pay more in order to provide dividends to the stockholders.

As part of this plan there would be a major effort undertaken to control and in some instances reduce healthcare costs. All healthcare costs would be thoroughly reviewed and excessive costs and price gouging eliminated. Fair and reasonable prices would be established for doctor visits, medical procedures and other areas of care. The practice of overcharging patients who have health insurance in order to pay for those patients who do not have health insurance would be stopped. Several years ago my wife went to a hospital in Florida to have a knee replacement. She takes several prescription drugs on an ongoing basis and keeps them in a small bag which she always has near her. Although she had her bag of medications right on the table next to her hospital bed the hospital refused to use her medications telling her that she had to use the hospital pharmacy. The bottom line is that she was charged $35 a day for a pill that she normally obtains for about 20 cents a day. I don't know how the hospitals are allowed to get away with this sort of thing. I also had a problem after she returned home when she received seven or eight separate invoices from various doctors on the hospital staff and other hospital personnel none of whom she recognized or even knew what they did. This is another practice that should be stopped and the rule should be that if someone is on the hospital staff they should be paid by the hospital. You do not spend a week in a hotel and come home and find a bill from the hotel chef or the desk clerk.

Perhaps the most important area of any major healthcare overhaul is to make certain that there are procedures in place that will insure that the highest standards of medical care will be provided. This includes improving the quality of our medical schools, the proper training of hospital personnel and making certain that doctors and hospitals have access to the latest medical equipment and that they are familiar with the most up to date medical procedures. Better training and higher standards of medical care would help reduce the number of patients who die every year from unintentional errors made by healthcare personnel.

The issue of healthcare is a vastly complex one and will require input from a number of different sources in order to find the correct solution. But the main points that must be understood by everyone are that government does not belong in the healthcare business and Medicare in its present form is headed for financial disaster. Those countries such as Canada and England that have experienced socialized medicine have been plagued with overcrowded doctors offices, long waiting periods for treatment and substandard care. In addition, there have been numerous instances where people over a certain age have been denied badly needed operations because it was felt that their remaining years would not justify using medical resources that could be better used for younger people. I don't think that we ever want to see the United States reach the point where a government agency has the power to determine who shall receive medical treatment and who shall not or to express this more dramatically to determine who shall live and who will die.

There is one other matter pertaining to healthcare that comes up often and that is the matter of people who do not have any health insurance. There are supposedly some 40 million plus Americans who do not have health insurance but I have never heard anyone identify these people and explain just who they are and why they do not have health insurance. I can think of three categories of people who might not have health insurance:

1. People with incomes below the poverty line who simply cannot afford healthcare insurance. But these are the same people who need food stamps, housing subsidies and other welfare benefits;

2. People who lose their jobs and no longer have the income to pay for healthcare insurance. There is such a thing as COBRA that gives someone who loses their job a certain period of time in which to continue with their health insurance provide they pay the premiums. I could never quite understand this because what is supposed to be a benefit comes at the worst possible time when the individual can least afford to pay for any insurance. I suggest that when a company lays off a worker that it should be the responsibility of the company to continue to pay the premiums on health insurance until the COBRA period expires;

3. There is a third group and this group consists of people who have more than sufficient income to pay for health insurance but who

for whatever reason decide not to purchase any. Maybe they want to use their money to take a trip around the world rather than buy health insurance or maybe they just want to gamble that they can go without insurance and that at the time they need it they will be able to purchase it.

The first two groups have a legitimate need for financial assistance in order to purchase health insurance. The third group should under no circumstances receive any aid to purchase insurance. I suggest that if government is going to provide assistance to those who do not have health insurance that it first examine the income level of the people they propose to assist. Those over a certain income level should not receive any assistance.

I am reminded of something that happened around the time of the Cuban Missile Crisis. My local newspaper had run an article about a man in Texas who announced that he was going to build a bomb shelter in his backyard. This may not have been so unusual in itself but what stirred up a controversy was when the man announced hat he was going to arm the bomb shelter with weapons in order to keep his neighbors out. The public became divided between those who said the man built the shelter on his own property with his own funds and had a right to keep out anyone he did not want. The other half said that the man had a moral obligation to offer his shelter to his neighbors even though they did not show the same foresight and built their own shelters. In any society there will always be a segment of the population that tries to coast along on the coattails and at the expense of someone else.

Of course when talking about healthcare regardless of who is running the system I think we have to conclude that no one should be denied proper healthcare under any circumstances. It is very annoying when the first thing you are asked when entering a doctor's office is what kind of insurance you have. Heaven help the individual who does not have health insurance. I know from first hand experience what this means. Several years ago my healthcare insurer came out with an option to convert to what turned out to be a Medicare advantage plan. I did not know the distinction at that time but the benefits seemed to be far greater and the premiums far less than on the insurance plan I currently had. Without thinking further I signed up for the advantage plan. A short time later I had an attack of painful gout in my right knee and went to the doctor who had been my primary physician for a number of years. I was told at the doctor's office that the doctor would not treat me because they did not accept Medicare advantage plans. I had to hobble out of the doctor's office in great pain to find another doctor who would accept this plan. Upon checking further I found that most of the doctors in my area would not accept these Medicare advantage plans and then requested and was allowed to convert back to the old insurance plan I previously had. It is unfortunate that what might have seemed like a beneficial idea in creating these Medicare advantage plans will not work if the doctors will not accept these plans.

While we are on the subject of healthcare it may be appropriate to have a short discussion regarding nursing homes. I don't think there is a country in the world that treats their elderly as poorly as we do in the United States. I have often heard people when talking about their elderly parents tell someone that "they have to find a place to put them." It is as if the elderly parents have some dreadful contagious disease and that they must be locked up someplace. This bothers me no end. There are people in the United States who treat their elderly parents like so much unwanted garbage. They just want to get rid of them. Putting someone into a nursing home is about the most degrading thing a person could do to someone. But to do it to someone's own parents is unforgivable.

In most countries the elderly are treated with veneration and respect and they are given a place of honor in the home. After all they have many years of wisdom and experience and the younger generations have much to learn from them. What is so terrible about having your elderly parents living in the same house with you? Some years ago my first wife's father who was ninety years old at the time fell and his doctor placed him in a nursing home for several weeks to convalesce. I recall visiting him one day. It was a very depressing experience. He was sharing a room with another elderly man. The room was sparsely furnished and they were not allowed any personal items. The room was one of many down a long corridor. At one end was a room where about a dozen women were sitting around watching a television set. I don't know what would happen if one of them wanted to change the channel. The other end of the corridor led into the main entrance hall and to my amazement it was kept locked and opened up only at meal times. The patients were being treated like prisoners in their rooms. On this particular day we were invited to stay for lunch. I remember asking a white-coated attendant standing near our table for some salt and pepper since there did not appear to be any on the table. I was promptly informed that none was available because the seasoning was put on the food in the kitchen. These poor people could not only not season their own food but they were also limited to what was served not otherwise having a menu to select from. How can we put our elderly in places like this and then go on about our own lives with a clear conscience?

I think the procedure that some states are now adopting makes all the sense in the world. That is to allow the elderly to remain in their own home and to provide a caretaker who will check up on and assist the individual when necessary. This is far less costly than the cost of a nursing home and provides the elderly individual with the dignity and comfort that can only be provided in their own home and familiar surroundings.

TOPIC III

EDUCATION

I recently saw an item in the newspaper that said that approximately $13,000 is spent annually on every school student in the United States. And yet the United States ranks far from the top in the world ranking of education. What is it that the Chinese and other Asian nations do that puts them at the top of the list? How much are they spending on education? We have much to learn from them. If the dollars spent on education in the United States were looked upon as an investment I am afraid they would have to be judged as producing a very low return.

The low ranking of American schools is very disappointing particularly considering the vast sums of money that are spent annually on the educational system. It is time that we took a closer look at the relationship between the dollars that are spent on education and the impact they have on scholastic achievement. Every town I have lived in and this goes back a good number of years seems to face the same debate every time a new school budget is proposed. The message always goes along the lines of getting more money or the children's education will suffer. The school budget process more often than not results in raising property taxes to provide the demanded funds. It is as if the property owners represent a vast pool of untapped resources that the school districts can just tap into whenever they want more money.

What people need to understand is that the dollars that are spent on education do not improve education per se. While it is not unusual for the school districts to receive the additional funds requested there is no mechanism in place that would require an improvement in a school's scholastic standing as a condition to receiving the additional funds. A substantial portion of every school budget goes for salaries and benefits for teachers, teachers assistants, school principals, administrative personnel and other school personnel. Most of the balance goes for operating and maintenance expenses. None of this directly translates into improving the quality of education. I am going to express this in a very simplistic manner but the only way a school's scholastic standing can be improved is for the teachers to teach more and the students to learn more. Spending more dollars on education in itself is not going to accomplish anything.

In any business employees are rewarded when the business does well. Perhaps if we set specific goals for each school and establish a system of bonus payments to teachers when these goals are exceeded it would go a long way to improving the quality of education in our schools and their overall scholastic ranking. Along with a system for rewarding teachers for improved results there should also be incentives to students to study hard and not drop out of school. Some type of cash reward should be handed out to those students who complete their school years and graduate as well as to those who achieve high scholastic standards. In the final analysis money talks and is the best incentive that can be provided. The combination of rewarding teachers for exceeding certain goals and rewarding students for certain achievements will do much to improve the scholastic ranking of all American schools. If these types of programs were in place they would justify the granting of additional funds.

One of the things I would like to see are more volunteers in the school system. Every community has retired individuals and local business people who have accumulated a wealth of knowledge and experience. If we could get some of these people to donate two or three hours a week of their time to helping out in classrooms it would bring an added dimension to the entire learning process. It would also have the benefit of bringing the students and the community closer together and allow the students to feel that there are people in the community who are genuinely interested in helping them.

An idea I have thought about for some time is the idea of placing all schools on a four day week. Instead of having a school end its day at 3:00 p.m. five days a week it would end its day at 5:00 p.m. four days a week. The savings in fuel costs alone from having the school buses operate four days instead of five would in themselves amount to hundreds of millions of dollars a year for school districts throughout the United States. There would also be substantial savings in heat and electricity as well as other savings from having the school buildings open one day less each week. But I would like to think that there is an even more important benefit from having the schools go to a four day week. That is an improvement in the morale of both students and teachers. The idea of having a three day weekend each week would in itself be a major benefit. It would give students an extra day to do their homework in a more leisurely less stressful manner. It might allow some to work at a part-time job for a few hours and make some extra money. And it would allow them to return to school at the beginning of the week ready to make a maximum effort having had three days off. The students might actually learn more since there would be a concentration of the school week into four days rather than five which would create a more intense and serious learning environment.

There is an obsession with many people that the most important thing upon graduating from high school is to get into a college. While there is nothing wrong with wanting to get a higher education the unfortunate thing is that many young people are stampeded into just any college that will accept them without giving any thought as to what they want to do with their life and whether that particular college is going to help them. The fact is that there are colleges and there are colleges and not all of them are equal and not all of them are viewed in the same light by prospective employers. There can be nothing worse than for a family to make a great financial sacrifice to send their son or daughter off to college only to find that the college lacks the standing they might have expected. To a student who just rushes off to any college that will accept them with the idea that it will be four years of fun and parties and excitement I say that it would be better to save your time and money for you are wasting your time.

Because the diplomas from so many colleges are viewed differently by different employers the risk to the college student is that they could waste four years of time and money and not have the opportunities that they might have thought would be open to them. Many of these individuals would do well to consider the advantages of attending a trade school or community college which are far less expensive than attending a four year college. Employers do recruit from these types of institutions and particularly in today's difficult job market this provides an opportunity to train for a specific skill for which there is a definite demand.

I recall an incident when I was working for an investment banking firm in New York City. Most investment banking firms are highly selective when it comes to recruiting young professionals and will consider only a few of the top ranked colleges and universities in the United States. In this particular incident the head of our corporate finance department brought me the resume from a young man who had just received a masters degree in business and wanted to get into investment banking. He was very proud of his accomplishments and further revealed that he had worked his way through college so that he could help support his family. Unfortunately the college where he received his masters degree was not considered one of the top colleges and the general feeling was that his degree could not be considered in the same light as a degree from one of the better colleges. While we liked this individual very much the decision was made not to hire him. I have always remembered this incident because it made me realize that the first thing anyone selecting a college must do is to determine what types of employers will hire graduates from that college.

One cannot discuss the Country's educational system without bringing the subject of sports into the picture. Now there is nothing wrong with sports which have become an increasingly important part of our national culture. But particularly among many colleges the obsession with sports has risen all out of proportion to what should be the primary function of any college namely education. This has led to all sorts of problems and abuses in recruiting athletes as well as other problems that have arisen and which have greatly damaged the reputation of many college athletic programs and in turn the reputations of the colleges themselves. There are dozens of colleges that excel in football or basketball and which have acquired a national reputation accordingly. It is rather revealing that many of these colleges will pay their football and basketball coaches multi million dollar salaries while their academic professors make only a small fraction of this amount. The fact is that sports have become big business at many colleges producing substantial revenues. There has even been some discussion as to whether or not college athletes should be paid a salary. Don't take this comment too seriously but it almost seems that where a college's athletic program is so successful and so profitable it might do better to just drop their academic function and concentrate solely on sports. Avid sports fans eagerly await the weekly rankings of college sports teams but they will never see a weekly ranking of academic standards. Anyone contemplating enrolling in one of these colleges would do well to thoroughly examine the success rate of the college's graduates in the job market before enrolling in the college. It is no secret that the heaviest recruiting done by Wall Street firms, the legal profession and the fortune 500 companies is from the ivy league colleges and perhaps a dozen or so other major colleges and universities and it is particularly significant that while all of these elite colleges and universities have athletic programs they do not place a disproportionate emphasis on sports.

A word about bullying. Bullying in schools probably dates back to when the first school opened. It is a terrible thing. When I went to school there were no school buses and everyone walked to school. I know the fear of looking down the street and seeing a group of bullies standing on a street corner. I used to have to take long detours around these groups just to avoid them. The problem is that someone who is bullied is often too embarrassed to mention it to their parents or teachers perhaps out of fear of retaliation from the bullies. I would encourage every school to make the elimination of bullying a top priority and to find ways to end it once and for all.

TOPIC IV

RETIREMENT

We need to adopt a uniform pension system in the United States one that will work the same way for every American regardless of where they work.

The Social Security system has on balance worked fairly well over the years. The benefits are clearly spelled out and people know in advance what they will be receiving depending upon the age at which they first start to drawn down benefits. This does have the disadvantage of putting people in the position of having to guess to how long they are going to live which no one can do with any degree of certainty. Just how long we will live and what the future holds is one of life's great unsolved mysteries. On my 64th birthday I went into the Social Security office in Hartford, Connecticut to see about applying for social security. I told the young woman who processed my application that I did not know whether I should start taking benefits now or whether I should wait until I was 65. This young woman who was very helpful pointed out that while I would receive somewhat higher payments if I waited until I was 65 if I started receiving payments at age 64 I would receive a full year of payments up front. The mathematics vary from individual to individual but if someone gets $900 a month at age 64 they will receive $10,800 by the time they are 65. If they wait until they are age 65 and receive $1,000 a month they will receive $1,200 a year more but it will take nine years to recover the $10,800 they otherwise would have received. Actually the breakeven point for most people works out to something round age 76 but as I mentioned this puts people in the position of having to gamble on how long they are going to live. Is this a good system where it is left up to the individual to try and guess how long they will live? Would it not be better to simply have one fixed retirement age for everyone and eliminate the guess work?

Another example of gambling on the future has to do with the small pensions I received from the two investment banking firms I worked for. I had a choice of receiving 100% of my pension amount but upon my death my wife would receive nothing. If I took a somewhat reduced pension amount this amount would continue to be paid to my wife as long as she lived. Given the always good health of my wife who was two years younger than me and given my heart history and the fact that the men in my family all died at a relatively young age it only made sense to me to provide some security for my wife. How was I to know that my wife would contract cancer and be dead within a short period of time leaving me with a reduced pension for the rest of my life?

The Social Security program has now reached the point where sometime in the not too distant future it will lack sufficient funds to meet its obligations. I am not certain just how it got to this point since Social Security was intended to be a self-financed program with the contributions from employees and their employers sufficient to cover the benefits paid out. Some points come to mind:

1. The Social Security budget should always be kept entirely separate from all other government budgets. It should not be co-mingled with the general budget. The Social Security budget should be

reviewed annually and when it is apparent that there would be a shortage of funds steps should be taken at that time to remedy the situation. It should never be allowed to get to the point where it is unable to meet its obligations;

2. The Social Security funds must be used solely for the intended purpose of providing benefits to the Social Security recipients. Under no circumstances should these funds be used for any other government purpose. The practice of government borrowing from these funds and issuing IOU notes must be stopped. A good comparison might be if government went into someone's private bank savings account and borrowed funds leaving an IOU note. When that individual went to their savings account to withdraw funds they would find only the IOU note;

3. Social Security must be reviewed periodically to insure that benefits are not being paid out to ineligible recipients. There is also a vast difference between someone who has worked for 40 years and contributed all that time and someone who is relatively new to Social Security and who has been contributing only a few years. The public has every right to know exactly how Social Security operates and who is getting benefits;

4. I would raise a fourth point and that is a request to the politicians in Washington to stop playing politics with the Social Security and Medicare programs. Everyone is aware that both these programs have serious financial problems. Just get down to the business of finding satisfactory solutions that will benefit the people who are supposed to be benefiting from them.

There are some who have been criticized for suggesting that Social Security is nothing more than a giant Ponzi scheme but in some respects the Social Security program does have the characteristics of a Ponzi scheme. However, fixing the potential financial problems of the Social Security program should be a fairly easy task. The first thing that needs to be determined in any pension system is what is a reasonable number of years to give to people for them to enjoy their retirement. Legend has it that it was Bismark of Germany who set the retirement age at 65. At that time life expectancy was around age 68 so this was giving people three years to enjoy their retirement. Even when our present Social Security program was enacted in the 1930s life expectancy wasn't much beyond this. These early pension systems were set up on the basis that people would have only a short time to live between the date they retired and their expected date of death. No one could have predicted at those times that people would be living until age 80 or 90 in the future. It is one thing to provide people with a pension for just a few years. It is a lot more costly to provide pensions for 20 or 25 years.

The way our Social Security program works is for a worker and their employer to make annual contributions based on a set percentage of the worker's pay up to a maximum ceiling. For someone who makes contributions for 40 years these contributions can add up. At the point the worker elects to begin receiving benefits they will receive a monthly check of some predetermined amount. If the worker were to live only a few years after beginning to receive these benefits their contributions would be more than enough to cover the amount they receive. However, because life expectancy has increased the chances are that the worker will outlive the contributions they have made. This means that in order to continue to pay benefits to the worker it is now necessary to use the contributions of workers who have yet to retire. When these workers eventually retire they find that a substantial portion of their contributions have already been used to continue to pay benefits to the retirees who have preceded them. It is then necessary for these workers to use the contributions of those who are still working to pay their benefits. When these later workers retire they will find little or nothing left of their contributions as they have been used up to support all those who have previously retired before them. This is what has the characteristics of a Ponzi scheme. Because the contributions made by each worker and their employer are not sufficient to pay the worker's benefits in full due to longer life spans each group of retirees will support the retirees before them and the last group to retire will find little or nothing left for them.

There are three things that can be done to save the Social Security program. The first is to raise the retirement age, the second is to reduce the benefits payable and the third is to increase the payroll contributions. I know of no other solutions. Raising the retirement age will affect current workers in the future. Reducing benefits will affect the current beneficiaries now and the current workers in the future. Increasing payroll contributions will affect current workers now. My solution is to raise the retirement age and eliminate the ceiling on income currently taxed. I suggest a retirement age of 70 be established. Since life expectancy is now around age 80 this would be giving people 10 years of retirement which is generous by any historical standards. Going to age 70 should probably begin in about 10 years in order to give people time to plan for a smooth transition into a higher retirement age. There should be no limit on the amount of income subject to the payroll tax. The tax rate should remain the same. While I am against raising income taxes on people just because they have a high income the Social Security payroll tax is in a different category. If we are going to have a Social Security program everyone should be treated in the same manner. This tax would be less onerous on someone making a million dollars a year than it is on someone making $40,000 or $50,000 a year. Having presented my solution to the Social Security problem I will now say that what I am really interested in would be the creation of a national pension system which I will discuss further.

There is little doubt that many government and public employees enjoy highly favorable benefits. Employees in the private sector do not fare as well. I was working in New York City back in the mid 1970s when the City had a financial crisis and announced that it might have to declare bankruptcy. The New York press began printing articles describing the generous benefit's the City's employees were receiving. The benefit that broke the City's back had to do with pensions. It seems that when a municipal worker retired they would receive a pension based on their total earnings the last year on the job which by definition included overtime pay. What happened was that an employee getting ready to retire would earn thousands of dollars of overtime pay their last year on the job and then retire on a huge inflated pension. We were reading about toll collectors who were making $100,000 their last year on the job before retiring. It was no wonder that the City approached bankruptcy. So desperate was New York City that it appealed to Washington for financial assistance. Gerald Ford was President at that time and he flatly refused to help the City. This prompted the New York Daily News to run probably the most famous front page that ever appeared in a New York newspaper printing in large letters "Ford to City: Drop Dead."

But President Ford was entirely correct in turning down the City's request. How could anyone justify using taxpayer dollars to bail out any municipality that entered into such a completely unreasonable and irresponsible agreement as the one that New York City did. To control the City's financial matters The State of New York set up a financial control board to take over the City's financial affairs which eventually brought financial stability.

We are beginning to become more and more aware of the serious financial difficulties various states and municipalities have got into resulting from these overly generous pension benefits which have been caused by employees making little or no contributions and by generous pensions being given at an early retirement age. Unfortunately not all Americans are so fortunate. There is nothing wrong with people getting highly favorable benefits. The problem is that the money is not always there to pay for them and as we are seeing this is placing a tremendous strain on the financial resources of these states and municipalities. This is why we need to change the entire pension system so that everyone is treated equally. Every worker regardless of where they work should be required to provide the same percentage of their wages into a common pension fund. The retirement age should be the same for everyone. The plan I am proposing would establish a uniform retirement age of 70.

What the United States needs is a national pension system that would not only replace and take over the current Social Security program but also replace and take over all current public and private pension plans. The objective would be to create the same rules and benefits for everyone. At the present time there is a patchwork quilt array of pension plans and benefits that exist among both the public sector and the private sector. The amounts contributed by employees, the ages at which they can retire and the amounts they receive vary all over the lot. Every employee should be required to have the same amount deducted from their paycheck and every employee should start receiving their pension at the same age.

As we know there is a serious unemployment problem in the United States. There are simply not enough jobs available and the population is increasing rapidly. Particularly among young people attempting to enter the labor force for their first job the situation has become acute. At the same time the older workers are trying to hold on to their jobs as long as they can. This creates a conflict between the younger workers and the older workers. Who is taking jobs from whom? At the same time there is talk about the present Social Security program running out of funds and the need to extend the retirement age and have people work longer. But this raises another problem as there is no guaranty that employers will allow older workers to stay employed. I recall back in the 1980s firms were terminating employees over age 50 left and right. I myself was part of this process and anyone who was over age 50 and had to find a job knows the frustration in finding out that nobody wanted to hire people over age 50. We cannot have it both ways. We cannot have government telling people that they should plan to work longer when employers do not want to have older people on their payrolls.

Essentially my plan would restructure the entire employment picture. I envision a two tiered employment system that would come in in two phases. The first phase would consist of a top tier of full time jobs that would be filled by people age 20 to age 50. At age 50 people would go into a semi-retirement status and there would be a second tier of part-time jobs that people age 50 to age 70 could fill. This would enable people to gradually phase into full retirement and they could work until age 70. The part-time job might very well be with the same employer the person had been working with in a full time capacity.

Every worker would contribute 10% of their wages into this national pension system and the employer would add an additional 10%. This would include both the public sector and the private sector and would be in lieu of the current Social Security contributions. This portion of wages would not be subject to income tax. At age 50 when someone went into semi-retirement they would begin to receive one-half the full pension amount that would be payable beginning at age 70. This coupled with their part-time wages would carry them through to age 70. At age 70 they would receive the full pension amount which would be the same for everyone. It would be up to each individual to determine whether they wanted to or needed to work part-time given their individual financial circumstances. There would also be an option that if someone wanted to continue to work part-time until age 75 they could defer their full pension and continue to receive half their pension. At age 75 they would receive a somewhat larger pension than they would otherwise have received at age 70.

The objective of this national pension system would be to allow older workers to work until age 70 in part-time jobs and at the same time open up more full-time employment opportunities for the younger workers. It would have a sense of fairness since all workers would be treated exactly the same. Of course any worker would be able on their own to the extent their finances allowed put aside additional funds for their retirement which they could invest privately.

Whether this plan whereby workers go into a semi-retirement status at age 50 in order to open up full time opportunities for younger workers is the answer would have to be determined. It should be given serious consideration because in the years to come the Country's population is going to increase tremendously. There will be an increasingly larger number of younger people who will be looking to enter the work force for the first time. Failure to have sufficient jobs for these young workers is a potentially serious problem. If things get bad enough it could have major social and political consequences. We must try to avoid this at all costs.

TOPIC V

ENERGY

As someone who lived through the oil crisis in the mid 1970s I can remember getting up at 5:00 o'clock in the morning to get gas and waiting for two hours in a line that went around the block hoping there would be some gas left by the time I reached the gas pump. We did not learn from this and did nothing to prevent similar problems from occurring in the future. Now a third of a century later we are still having problems with oil. The price has risen at times to over $100 a barrel and gasoline has approached $4.00 a gallon. I do not know why we allow ourselves to be so dependent on and affected by the various oil producing countries. What I would like to do is to end our dependence on foreign oil once and for all and make oil practically obsolete going the way of the covered wagon.

One of the negative impacts of importing so much oil is the effect on our trade balance of payments. The last time I looked at the exports and imports there was a huge trade deficit caused entirely by the payments made for importing oil. If we were to take oil out of the picture there would be a trade surplus. We cannot allow this trade deficit to go on year after year.

I remember back in the 1970s and 1980s the number of electric utility companies that wanted to build nuclear power plants but which were thwarted by politicians who were vehemently opposed to nuclear power. The resulting regulatory delays not only added years to the construction schedules of these plants but also added hundreds of millions of dollars to the total cost. Many of these projects were simply abandoned. This short sightedness on the part of these politicians would eventually cause billions of dollars to be spent as costly oil had to be imported to make up for the loss of what would otherwise have been low cost nuclear power.

While I am certain that many people may disagree for various reasons I am a strong advocate that our future lies in the expansion of nuclear power. We are now living in the 21st century and it is time we took full advantage of the atom and get all the benefits we can from it. I know there have been several major disasters involving nuclear power plants over the years one of which was in the United States but the fact is that the nuclear power industry has a safety record unmatched by any other industry. There are more accidents in one year alone from airplane accidents, oil drilling accidents, coal mining accidents, natural gas explosions and almost any industry you can name than there have been in 55 years of nuclear power plant operation. In fact, the fatalities from nuclear power plant accidents over this time period are practically nil. The nuclear power plants that have been operating in the United States have been able to withstand every natural phenomenon including floods, hurricanes, tornados and earthquakes without incurring any major damage and without any serious injuries or fatalities. By any standards the safety record of the nuclear power industry is one that any other industry can envy.

I am proposing a 10 year crash program at the end of which 50% of our total energy requirements would be provided by nuclear power. The energy mix that I propose would be nuclear 50%, natural gas 15%, coal 15%, hydro 10% and other sources including oil, windmills and solar

10%. The use of oil would be primarily for the airlines industry, military use and some industrial use. These requirements would be relatively small in relation to our total energy requirements and could be provided entirely from our own domestic production. It would never be necessary to import a single barrel of oil again. There are those who would like to see sources of energy such as windmills and solar developed but I would point out that these sources can provide only very limited amounts of energy and are not really cost effective. And they need back up power. Rather than use funds to develop these sources of energy the funds would be better applied to the construction of large base load nuclear generating units capable of producing tremendous amounts of power.

This energy plan is designed to accomplish the following:

1. To provide the United States with an abundant supply of clean dependable low cost electric power;
2. To eliminate the need to import a single barrel of foreign oil;
3. To stimulate local economies and reduce unemployment. The potential is to create two to three million jobs including the construction workers, the parts and materials suppliers and the local businesses that would see increased activity because of the benefits from having the power plants constructed in their area;
4. It would improve environmental air pollution by allowing the automobile industry to fully convert to electric automobiles.

I envision a quasi government agency that would finance and operate these nuclear power plants modeled somewhat after the Tennessee Valley Authority with some modifications. The plan involves building 20 to 25 large base load nuclear generating units each having as large a capacity as the engineering technology will allow at least one million kilowatts plus. To avoid problems with local regulatory agencies these plants would be built on federal lands as close to large population centers as safety would permit but not so close as to provide a hazard in the unlikely event something were to happen. This might increase the transmission cost slightly but this would be offset by the lower cost power generated by the unit.

The financing of these nuclear power plants would consist of 70% debt and 30% equity. The debt would consist of power revenue bonds secured by a first lien on the revenues from the sale of power which would be sold under long term take or pay contracts. The interest would be exempt from all federal, state and local taxes. The bonds would be guilt edge, triple A rated and guaranteed by the United States Government. Accordingly they would be one of the safest investments in the world and would carry a relatively low rate of interest which in turn would lower the cost of the power sold. The bonds would be sold worldwide thus enabling a major portion of the financing to be provided by foreign investors. The equity portion of 30% would be provided 5 % by the federal government, 12 1/2% by the purchasers of the power which would include both public and private electric utility systems and large industrial users with the remaining 12 ½% set aside for the sale of stock to the general public. Because the power would be sold to the purchasers under long term take or pay contracts and the debt interest would be relatively low the rates for power would be low enough to still allow for a decent return on the common stock equity. Accordingly the common stock would have more of the characteristics and stability of a preferred stock. I envision dividends being paid on this stock that would produce a return of around 6% thereby making it a very safe and dependable investment sort of placing it into the old widows and orphans category.

This agency would be controlled by a board of ten directors of which two would be appointed by the federal government, four would be appointed by the purchasers of the power and four would be elected by the general public stockholders. The day to day operations would be handled by those companies in the private electric industry that have the most expertise in the area of nuclear power generation.

As part of this plan the automobile industry would be converted 100% over to the electric automobile. The manufacture of gasoline powered cars would be phased out over a three year period and at the end of ten years when the nuclear plants start producing and selling electricity gasoline powered cars would begin to be phased off the highways and this phase out would be completed within another three years.

It has taken a long time for the electric automobile to begin to be accepted. The idea has been around for decades. I can remember in the 1950s when the Chairman of the Union Electric Company of St. Louis, Missouri came to New York City and talked about the electric automobile and the possibilities it offered at a meeting of financial analysts. Unfortunately the idea progressed very slowly.

Some people are concerned about the batteries in electric automobiles and wonder about the mileage one gets from a fully charged battery and the length of time it takes to recharge the battery. I am certain that our engineers have the knowledge and ability to solve these problems and that they will be able to create batteries that will provide greater mileage and also batteries that can be fully recharged in a relatively short period of time.

Not being an engineer I probably should not attempt to get too carried away in my ideas of what might be feasible but I have several ideas as to how the battery problem might be solved:

1. If the battery cannot be recharged in a short time say ten minutes or so one option would be for every car to carry two batteries. When the first battery runs down the second battery could easily be installed. Assuming that one battery has a life of approximately

250 miles this would allow around 500 miles of driving before the two batteries would have to be recharged;

2. Another option would be for all service stations to carry an inventory of fully charged batteries. When a battery needs to be recharged the driver would merely drive into a service station and the attendant would replace the run down battery with a fully charged battery much the same way that the owner of a gas grill exchanges an empty cylinder of propane for a full one;

3. The innovation I like the best and I am certain that it is not impossible would be to have three batteries installed in the car with a control panel on the dash board. When the first battery runs down the driver would merely push a button and battery number two would take over. And the same with battery number three. The best of all worlds would be if the engineers could develop a self charging battery so that when the first battery runs down it would be recharging while battery number two takes over.

I do not think that what I am proposing is impossible to achieve and the benefits will be tremendous. It may be difficult at first for the American people to accept the idea of the electric powered automobile but it is something that they will get used to and they will soon realize how much better off they are. Replacing expensive gasoline with low cost electricity will reduce driving costs substantially. When the American people have to adjust to something they will adjust. After all who would have predicted 40 years ago that the day would come when people would be pumping their own gasoline at a service station

TOPIC VI

SOCIAL ISSUES

Some of the major domestic issues facing the American people today have to do with issues such as abortion and gay marriages. It is unfortunate that these "social" issues have become so divisive and are exploited to the extent they are by the politicians. The biggest challenge for the American people is to determine the dividing line between where an individual's right to make these highly personal decisions leaves off and government's right to interfere begins. But beware! Like the proverbial camel that stuck its nose into the tent once government intrudes into an individual's personal decisions there will be no turning back and the individual will soon find out that they no longer have any control over any aspect of their life.

The standards of morality in the United States should be determined only by the American people themselves without any external influence. No organization or individual should attempt to preach morality to the American people. Issues like abortion and gay marriages should be decided by the voters of each state on a state by state basis without any outside influence. It should be entirely up to the people in those states. This could result in different standards being adopted by different states but if this is the will of the people in those states then so be it.

America was founded on the principle of separation of church and state and it is somewhat interesting to see some politicians campaigning before religious groups in an attempt to get their support. What this is doing is to potentially allow the views and influence of a particular religious organization to be imposed on all the people beyond the membership of that religious organization which is contrary to the principle of separation of church and state. I am very surprised that for this reason the American people have not requested that politicians stop attempting to curry favor with religious organizations. Religion has a definite place in our society but religion and politics should never mix.

A good example of government intrusion into personal decisions has to do with wearing a seat belt. Wearing a seat belt may make good sense in most instances but this is something that each individual should be able to decide for themselves. Whenever I hear that the police are starting a crackdown on seat belt violators my immediate reaction is that it is a terrible misuse of police time which ought to be devoted to going after more serious crime. The whole idea of government requiring seat belt use would seem to be simply a way for government to gain more power and control over the population and it probably raises substantial amounts of money from fines imposed for not wearing a seat belt. But why do we need to have government telling us that we must wear a seat belt in the first place? This sort of thing is only the beginning if the people let it get out of hand. And apparently it is not 100% effective anyway despite the efforts to enforce the law. I suggest that a more effective way of enforcing seat belt use would have been for the automobile insurance companies to simply say that they would not pay any claims if someone was not wearing a seat belt. I am certain this would cause people to think twice.

Government intrusion into personal decisions has even attempted to wade into the issue of assisted suicides. I have always felt that there are two things necessary if a person is going to be comfortable in their old age and enjoy life as they should. They need money and they need good health. But what about those who do not have sufficient financial resources or those whose health has deteriorated beyond any reasonable standards? I know that I would not want to be kept alive under those circumstances. They say that death is harder on the living but no one should have to experience a living death. Of course if someone has a living will it should take care of most of these situations. But where a living will does not exist the final decision as to whether or not to attempt to keep someone alive should be between the individual's doctor and their next of kin and government should stay out of it.

Perhaps the most inflammatory and divisive issue is the issue of abortion. It is probably the most divisive issue confronting the American people since the issue of slavery 150 years ago. I am convinced that if the pro life and pro choice segments of the population were separated geographically north and south or east and west there would long ago have been another civil war over this issue. All forms of life are precious whether they be human, animal or plant. I am certain everyone agrees on this and to destroy any living thing is the greatest crime anyone can commit.

I have never seen any reliable polls that would provide an accurate number of the pro life and pro choice supporters. If I had to guess I would say that the pro life supporters outnumber the pro choice supporters but have no way of knowing by how much other than there would appear to be a large number of supporters for each side of the abortion question. It is absolutely essential that some compromise be reached that will be fair to each group and which most importantly will put this issue to rest once and for all. We cannot go on year after year debating the issue of abortion.

The compromise that I would propose is something along the lines of giving a woman 30 days after becoming pregnant to decide whether or not to abort the pregnancy and after 30 days making all abortions illegal.

There would of course have to be some exceptions such as when the life of the mother is at risk or when it is determined that the fetus has grown into a grotesque or deformed state but this is the general idea. I call this the 30 day rule.

I know there are a lot of people who support the definition of marriage as being between a man and a woman and there certainly is nothing wrong with this. Putting the bible and gay marriages aside the concept of marriage being between a man and a woman is a very nice quaint notion. After all there are thousands of married couples each year who celebrate their golden wedding anniversary and who have faithfully honored their marriage vows over the years. Unfortunately, not all marriages between a man and a woman are so fortunate as to fall into this category.

Those who feel so strongly that marriage should be between a man and a woman should consider a few facts not the least of which is the high rate of divorce. There are millions of cases each year of spousal abuse with husbands assaulting their wives and wives assaulting their husbands. There are millions of broken homes as a result of alcohol, drugs and gambling with devastating effects on the children. And there are millions of instances of marital infidelity husbands cheating on their wives and wives having affairs with someone else. Is this that perfect type of relationship that those who advocate that marriage should be between a man and a woman want to create? I know that I would not be happy about living next door to a man and wife who were always fighting with the dishes continuously flying out the window. It is not the purpose of this book to take a position on gay marriages one way or the other or even attempt to define what constitutes a normal marriage but I think that those who advocate that marriage should be between a man and a woman need to do a little soul searching and try to figure out how to improve these relationships.

One encouraging development has been the number of men and women who live together prior to actually getting married. While at one time these kinds of relationships would have been considered taboo they have the benefit of giving a couple the opportunity of getting to know one another and deciding whether they are right for each other before they actually tie the knot and it is too late. This may be helpful in reducing the divorce rate.

As for gay marriages it should not be left up to the Federal Government to decide their fate. This is a matter for each individual state to decide. Each state should have a statewide referendum on the question and the outcome of that referendum should be decisive. It is entirely possible that the Country could eventually end up with half the states legalizing gay marriages and half the states disallowing them. Probably in 20 or 30 years gay marriages will have become accepted to the point that people will look back and wonder what all the fuss was about. This issue is no different than the fight to get women the vote or the fight to get women into the work force or the advances in civil rights. All of these crusades took time as they are not the sort of matters that are conducive to quick public acceptance.

Just why are there so many extramarital affairs and is there really anything wrong with engaging in one? I think the bar was lowered when a former President of The United States had an illicit sexual encounter with another woman and the general reaction seemed to be so what it is business as usual and the President was allowed to remain in office. If the American people are going to allow a President of The United States to have an illicit sexual encounter and simply go about his business as if nothing happened they are then establishing the standard for Mr. and Mrs. average American to follow. Under no circumstances should there be a double standard. Perhaps the best answer I heard was when a former governor was having an affair with an Argentine woman. I just happened to be watching the evening news on television one night and there was a reporter in Argentina who was interviewing people on the street. He asked one woman what she thought of an American governor coming to Argentina to have an affair. She looked at the reporter and with a straight face told him that the Argentine women have a lot to offer. This left me wondering just what it was that the Argentine women have to offer that the American women do not have.

Whether people want to admit it or not the United States has become a sex conscious country. Sex is everywhere in newspapers, magazines, books, movies, television, advertising you name it and sex is there. We applaud a 90 year old couple when we hear that they engaged in sex. We give out condoms to high school children. We encourage slim and sexy body figures. Women will spend thousands of dollars to have their face lifted or have a breast implant. Topless bars have become big business and the internet is full of web sites catering to every type of sexual desire. One dating service I looked at showed over 100,000 women looking for women and over 100,000 men looking for men. It is no wonder that people build up fantasies in their minds being continuously exposed to all this. At some point they have to have a release.

Many of the publicized instances of extramarital affairs involve men who work hard and who are highly successful and prominent in business or government. Of course there are many more extramarital affairs involving plain ordinary men that simply are not newsworthy. And even though women have extramarital affairs they are rarely subjected to the same publicity that a man would be subjected to. I suspect that in the majority of instances the men who engage in these extramarital affairs are devoted to their families and the last thing they are thinking about is breaking up their family relationship. In fact, they look upon their success as enabling their family to enjoy a better lifestyle. What they are seeking is a satisfaction that they cannot obtain at home. A man cannot come home after a hard day's work and expect to find his wife standing at the door dressed in a black leather outfit and holding a whip while the children play merrily on the living room floor.

There is no question that in the last 50 or 60 years the standards of morality in the United States have been greatly lowered. I think of the movie "Gone With the Wind" when Clark Gable shocked the audience by uttering the word "damn." Nowadays few movies are made that do not have a liberal sprinkling of choice four letter words as apparently the producers feel that this is good box office and the same may be said for the frequency of sex and violence. And the movie producers are usually pretty good judges of what the American people want. This along with the relaxation of sexual standards generally indicates that we are now living in a very liberal society almost to the point where anything goes. We may not be quite at the point where we will become another Sodom and Gomorrah but if the standards of morality continue to be lowered who knows what might happen in the future.

I am not going to get into a discussion about illegal drugs. There are arguments both for and against their legalization. I do realize that as long as the use of drugs is considered illegal it probably gives employment to thousands of people who would otherwise be out of a job if the use of drugs were legalized. These would include judges, prosecutors, attorneys, law enforcement officers and prison guards and officials. It was Samuel Insull of public utility fame who once said that if he had walked down the street in 1932 carrying a bottle of whiskey in one hand and a bar of gold in the other he would be arrested for carrying the whiskey but in 1933 he would have been arrested for carrying the gold. With the stroke of a pen something that is illegal one year can be made legal the next.

Speaking of whiskey I have just finished watching the series on Prohibition that was shown on public television. I thought this was an excellent series that fairly presented both sides of the problem. Through hindsight the law never should have been passed in the first place and fortunately the American people had the good sense to get the law repealed. But as someone said when ten percent of the population creates a problem you do not pass a law that impacts the other ninety percent. You address the problems of the ten percent. I used to enjoy one or two drinks every night before dinner until my doctor diagnosed me with CLL and said I should give up alcohol. I always enjoyed Canadian Club. I really liked scotch but the only time I could afford it was when I could charge it off as a business expense. My doctors have all said that an occasional glass of red wine is beneficial and I now drink one or two glasses every evening. I drink Carlo Rossi burgundy which is good enough for me and all I can afford. I am not a connoisseur and could not tell the difference between a $100 bottle of wine and a bottle of grape juice.

I would like to comment briefly on the use of steroids by athletes. I may be displaying my ignorance but I fail to see why this is considered such a crime. That the United States Congress would waste taxpayer dollars investigating this is beyond me. I grew up in the 1940s listening to Jack Armstrong on the radio and I still remember the message to get plenty of fresh air, sleep and exercise and eat plenty of Wheaties. I learned that it is the responsibility of every athlete to do everything they can to develop a strong body to enhance their performance. This includes special diets, exercising, jogging and doing whatever is necessary to keep strong and fit. The use of steroids is just one more component of this process and if this makes the athlete stronger and better why should anyone criticize it? In fact, the finger might be pointed to those athletes who do not use steroids and the question asked why don't they? Should we place an asterisk next to the athlete who jogs five miles a day while the average for other athletes is to jog only two miles a day? Why should we penalize the individual who simply wants to become better and more successful? This in my opinion is just another instance where government is trying to intervene in someone's personal decisions. It should be entirely up to each athlete to weigh the pros and cons of using steroids and the decision of whether or not to use them should be left entirely to each athlete.

A few words about how business is conducted. When I first started working in the 1950s we did not have word processing machines, computers, copy machines, cell phones or voice mail. In fact the building I worked in did not even have air conditioning. But in spite of all this business was conducted in a highly successful manner. The biggest difference from today was that business was done on a highly personal basis through personal contacts and face to face meetings. A person's word was their bond and a deal was sealed with a handshake. Today many people seem to think that a job is simply sitting in front of a computer all day and punching data into it. They have lost the personal touch. It used to be that when you telephoned someone you got either the person you were calling on the phone or their secretary who would take a message and always get back to you. It was not like today where you get someone's voice mail and they may or may not return the call or having to listen to a robot recite a lengthy menu of items to you before you can even mention what you are calling about. We have certainly lost something over the years in the way business is conducted. Most of the time now you do not even know who you are talking to.

Along with the deterioration in the way business is conducted has been the trend toward casual attire for the office. For 30 years I wore a three piece suit, a white shirt and tie and black dress shoes to work. About the time I left in the mid 1980s the novelty of a casual Friday came into being. People like myself were shocked at this new trend and had difficulty accepting it. Now the trend to casual wearing apparel has spread to the entire work week. When I see the way some of the people waiting in lines at some of the job fairs are dressed I realize that one of the things that keeps people from getting hired is that they simply do not know how to dress for business.

I recall about 15 years ago being summoned for jury duty in Connecticut. It was a hot day in June and there were 40 or 50 people summoned. I was the only person wearing a suit and tie. Everyone looked as if they were planning a trip to the beach. As it turned out two cases were settled at the last moment and there was a surplus of jurors. Accordingly, they placed all the names in a hat and dismissed those whose names were called out. My name was the first name called. I was somewhat disappointed because I would have liked to have been around to see the reaction of the judge when he saw how everyone was dressed.

Just so I do not leave anyone with the wrong impression I will say that since I have been retired I have not worn a suit and tie for over 10 years and the only suit in my closet is over 20 years old and would fit me like a tent if I attempted to wear it.

TOPIC VII

THE MILITARY

My grandmother used to say that if all wars were fought by men in their 50s and 60s there would never be any wars. When we listen to veterans in their 70s, 80s and 90s talk about the prior wars they fought in it is sometimes hard to realize that when they were actually fighting in those wars they were 18, 19, 20, 21, 22 years old. Someone in their late 20s would be considered the old man of a unit. The men who made the invasion landings, the men who flew the bombing raids and the men who sailed the ships at sea were merely young boys that the ordeal of war turned into battle hardened men overnight. I think the toughest decision that any President has to make is when to send the young men of American into war. To me it is such a heart wrenching decision knowing that thousands will be killed or wounded and we often have to question was it worth the price we had to pay. It is difficult to imagine what goes on in the minds of brave young Americans when they are in a landing craft preparing to storm a beach knowing that in a matter of minutes half of them will be killed. Their courage is unmatched only by their patriotism. The American public back in the comfort of their own homes rarely knows at the time the ordeal that our military is being subjected to. I am still learning after all these years some of the horrors that our prisoners of war were subjected to during World War II. The phrase "war is Hell" is one of the great understatements of all time.

Since the beginning of the 20th Century the United States has been involved in numerous major wars including World War I, World War II, the Korean War, the Vietnam War, the first Iraq War and the more recent Iraq and Afghanistan Wars. It almost seems that each war has dragged on longer than the ones before it and with each war the American people have become less interested and supportive of the war effort. And it might be added that with each war our military effort seems to be less effective. Certainly during World War I and World War II patriotism and support for the war effort was at the highest level. The entire Country was united and in each instance our military emerged victorious. The Korean War was a hard fought war under very difficult conditions and our military performed in an outstanding manner in spite of the numerous hardships that had to be overcome. Rather than have a military ending the war had a political ending as our government was afraid of the war escalating beyond Korea itself. We did accomplish the objective of keeping the North Koreans out of South Korea. I have never considered myself a hero because the 13 months I spent in Korea began one month after the fighting stopped in 1953. I simply did my job and would never place myself in the same category as the brave men who did the actual fighting and suffered the hardships before the fighting ended. When it came to the Vietnam War the Country had become so opposed to war that it gave rise to draft dodging and numerous demonstrations. Unless someone was directly affected by the war people just went about their business as usual.

I would like to digress for just a moment and mention my impression of the officers I encountered while serving in the Army recognizing that this was almost 60 years ago. I was an enlisted man assigned to a headquarters unit in Taegu, Korea. The ratio of enlisted personnel to officers was about two to one that is there were about 400 enlisted personnel and 200 officers. I don't know if our unit was an exception or not but there was very little of what you might call strict military protocol. The entire atmosphere was rather relaxed and informal. The officers had an almost paternalistic relationship with the enlisted personnel. It was more like a father and son relationship. The officers looked after their men and were always ready to assist them with any problems they might have had. Practically all of these officers were regular army career officers. A better description of them might be to classify them as gentlemen rather than military officers. But they all had one thing in common. Their first rule was to never do or say anything that was in the least way controversial and that would create waves and rock the boat. They all knew how to play the system and survive in the military bureaucracy. I recall one instance when a 50 year old first lieutenant was assigned to the unit. He had been in grade a number of years and had reached the point where if he did not get promoted within a relatively short period of time his army career would be over. Within three months they had found a way to get him promoted to captain. As I say they all knew how to play the game and survive in the system.

While the United States may have been fully justified in participating in World War I, World War II, the Korean War and the Vietnam War our involvement in Iraq and Afghanistan has been the subject of much debate both for and against. I find it hard to believe that in 10 years we have been unable to put a stop to what seem to be daily attacks on our military forces. The United States is supposed to have the most powerful military force in the world and yet we can not stop a few thousand terrorists from continuously committing violence and havoc. What is wrong here? I would like someone to explain this to me. It would appear from the way things have been going that this could continue on indefinitely. In most wars the war is fought with a definite objective in sight and a plan to end the war as quickly as possible. To enter into an open ended type of war with no end in sight just does not make any sense.

I think of the way the Germans blitzed their way through country after country during World War II often taking only weeks or months to achieve total victory. Any rebellions or uprisings were quickly put down. Of course the Germans used extreme and harsh measures but they were usually effective. I am convinced that if we had a million troops in Afghanistan the only result would be that we would have ten times the casualties we currently have. We are not fighting a nation across an open battlefield where planes, tanks, artillery and millions of troops will determine the outcome. This is an entirely different kind of war where the enemy suddenly appears out of nowhere strikes and then disappears just as quickly. It is a subversive almost invisible type of war and what is required is greater exchange of intelligence, infiltration of terrorist cells, informants and perhaps a bounty system and most importantly greater defense of our boarders and the monitoring of suspicious behavior. All the tanks and planes in the world or a million troops are not going to stop a suicide bomber who blends in with 20 others on a street corner and looks the same as everyone else

I think we might have done better had we pulled all our troops out of Afghanistan and formed a strike force along with our allies of perhaps 50,000 troops. This force would be ready to act on a moments notice and at the point the enemy came out into the open and attempted to take over the country this force could then go in having definite targets to strike. This in my opinion would be far more effective than subjecting our troops to the daily hazards of facing an invisible enemy.

The price the United States has paid for ten years of fighting in Iraq and Afghanistan has been very steep. Thousands of decent, patriotic young Americans killed, tens of thousands wounded many with terrible life long injuries, hundreds of billions of dollars spent. I doubt that the cost in lives and dollars incurred by the forces we have been fighting have been any more than a small fraction of the cost the United States has incurred. And after ten years bombs are still going off and people are still being killed and American casualties are still mounting. If it were up to me I would have pulled our military forces out of these countries long ago. As I have indicated there are better and more effective ways of dealing with these terrorist forces. One American casualty is one casualty too many. And if I were President the first thing I would do would be to turn the Camp David retreat over to the Veterans Administration to be used as a convalescent center for the most severely wounded war veterans and their families to spend some time where they could receive top medical care and enjoy a restful environment to ease their transition from military life back to civilian life.

Our military successes in the different wars our Country has fought have been in direct relationship to the amount of public support received. As public apathy grows our military effort is less successful. In both World War I and World War II the entire nation rallied around the war effort. Men were drafted, women worked in defense plants, people bought war bonds and the entire Country was united in its support of the armed forces. What the United States did in World War II was in my opinion the most magnificent accomplishment that has been achieved during my lifetime. When you stop and think about it all we did was to flex our powerful muscles and bring our united strength to bare on two of the most powerful and sinister militaristic countries the world had ever known each of which had been preparing for war a for a decade before we even entered into it. That we were able to finish off both of these enemies in three and a half years or so was nothing short of a miracle. Winston Churchill said of the English people during the Blitz of London in 1940 that it was their finest hour. I would have to say that the years 1941 to 1945 and the way the American people rallied together were America's finest hour. It is also remarkable that we have been able to put behind us Japan's treacherous attack upon Pearl Harbor and their heinous and brutal treatment of our military personnel with the result that Japan is now one of our staunchest allies. Most of the credit for this should go to Douglas MacArthur for the way he handled the surrender of Japan and his subsequent administration of post-war Japan.

Now I know the women of America are going to jump all over me and I respect their right to do so but nevertheless I will say that in my opinion it is absolutely wrong to have women serving in combat roles. There is such a thing as going too far in creating a politically correct military force. That is not to say that women cannot make a tremendous contribution in non-combat roles because the records shows that they have distinguished themselves in all wars in which they have participated. Perhaps this is nothing more than some southern chivalry rubbing off on me since I moved to North Carolina which causes me to believe that women should never be exposed to the hazards of combat.

I do not think that the United States should be the world's policeman and carry the load every time there is an uprising someplace. With the exception of our loyal British friends those countries that have supported us have for the most part provided relatively limited numbers of troops. The first and foremost responsibility of our military forces should be to defend our Country from any attacks. We cannot defend the world by ourselves. If this later course is what the American people want then there must be a resolute will to make the necessary sacrifices. This would include instituting a military draft so that sufficient manpower would be available. Since the Vietnam War the idea of a military draft has been soundly rejected by the American people and no politician would risk their career even suggesting the idea. This leaves us with the national guard. I have always been under the impression that the primary purpose of the national guard is to perform domestic duties. I have never thought of it as being a permanent replacement for the regular army and it seems very unfair to assign the national guard units to two and three tours of duty simply because we lack the sufficient manpower of a regular army.

While our military forces may be relatively small for the many tasks required of it around the world it is made up of dedicated patriotic Americans who perform their role in an exemplary manner. And we do have a solid core of highly specialized units and special forces consisting of dedicated and well trained men and women who have performed some extraordinary feats. We owe a lot to these individuals. The only question is whether we have enough of them.

It is highly doubtful that the United States will ever again be engaged in a full scale war such as World War II, Korea or Vietnam. If such a war were ever to break out it would probably mean a nuclear holocaust and no nation wants to take that risk. When the United States dropped the two atomic bombs on Japan in August, 1945 it accomplished several things. It brought the war to a quick end. It saved countless lives on both sides some estimate upwards of one million and it to some extent was a pay back to the Japanese for their attack on Pearl harbor, the Bataan death march, the brutal treatment of prisoners of war and the many atrocities they committed. But perhaps the biggest contribution to mankind and humanity was that it showed the world what a terrible and destructive weapon it was. In the subsequent 66 years while many nations now have atomic weapons which are many times more powerful than the original bombs dropped on Japan no nation has been foolish enough to even contemplate using any atomic weapons.

I cannot end this discussion of the dropping of the atomic bombs without mentioning the matter of Captain McVay who commanded the USS Indianapolis. Captain McVay was charged with the mission of delivering vital components of the first atomic bomb to our airbase at Tinian a mission which he successfully fulfilled. This as much as anything led to the ending of the war in the Pacific. Captain McVay is one of America's true heroes and deserves the highest honor and recognition. The subsequent sinking of the Indianapolis and the disgraceful trial of Captain McVay is one of the darkest moments in the history of the United States Navy and has been well documented. The reason I bring this up is that I have observed over the years that whether it is in government, the military or even in the corporate world there is a tendency for those who are responsible at the highest levels to attempt to cover up their own roles when something goes wrong and to look for a lower echelon scapegoat to whom they can shift the blame. This was certainly the case with Captain McVay and I have the highest respect for President Clinton for his exoneration of Captain McVay.

It disturbs me somewhat when I hear the politicians and news media people talk about some of the smaller countries around the world that are attempting to develop nuclear weapons. It almost seems that these people get great satisfaction from trying to instill fear into the American people as if we are supposed to shake and tremble at the prospect. My response to this is that the American people have nothing to fear. In fact, it is the population of these countries that should go to bed at night praying that their government never attempts any thing so foolish because if any country ever attempted to use an atomic weapon or if it ever provided atomic weapons to any terrorist group that attempted to use them the retaliation would be so swift, so terrible and so complete it would have the effect of literally wiping that country off the map. And I think these countries know this.

TOPIC VIII

POLITICS

Our political system is a democratic one essentially based upon a two party system namely the Democratic Party and the Republican Party. There are numerous smaller or splinter parties that from time to time have offered some outstanding candidates but these candidates have always run in futility with little chance of getting elected. This is unfortunate because some of these third party candidates might have done a better job of solving the Country's problems had they been elected. The American people have a strange habit of often voting for the wrong candidate for the wrong reasons. Or to put it another way for unknown reasons they will often reject a candidate who shares their views and who would have made a better elected official and end up voting for someone who turns out to be rather mediocre.

I think back to the Presidential Election in 1960 that was one of the closest in history. Had Richard Nixon been elected rather than John Kennedy who knows what the course of our history would have been. How would Richard Nixon have handled the Cuban Missile Crisis assuming it would have even occurred? Probably we would never have gone to war in Vietnam and the Watergate incident would certainly never have occurred.

In 1964 the people had an opportunity to elect Barry Goldwater but instead elected Lyndon Johnson. In 1976 they had an opportunity to re-elect Gerald Ford but instead elected Jimmy Carter. And in 2008 the people elected Barack Obama over John McCain. There is no way of knowing how much better off the Country would have been if these losing candidates had been elected instead. But the point is that rather than always use their best judgment the American people are often stampeded into voting for someone for the wrong reasons and then regretting their decision when it is too late to restore the damage. I leave it up to the American people to decide whether or not Goldwater, Ford and McCain would have made better presidents and whether the Country would have been better off than under the administrations of Johnson, Carter and Obama.

There needs to be a better way of conducting campaigns for political office. We have reached point where the entire process has come down to which candidate can raise and spend the most money. This should not be the criteria for determining who is best qualified for the office. Nor should the public be influenced by the polls appearing in the press, the editorial comments of the press or even the speeches by the candidates themselves. In all my years no one has ever asked me for my opinion in connection with a Presidential poll and I have no idea whose opinions these polls are reflecting. I also think that the televised Presidential debates are a complete waste of time and prove nothing. There is nothing worse than seeing a group of potential candidates tearing each other apart in front of millions of viewers. What kind of an impression do you think that makes? Those candidates who run their campaigns in a negative manner trying to run down their opponents will never receive my vote. What I want to hear is a positive campaign and finding out what the candidate thinks he can accomplish and what his vision is for the office he is running for. When a candidate spends most of the time attempting to downgrade their opponent it tells me this is not the kind of person we should be electing. We need to bring the highest ethical standards and civility into politics. We need more statesmen and fewer politicians. I have said it before and I will say it again that the American people need to stand on their own two feet and think for themselves when deciding who to vote for.

In 2008 the pendulum swung to the left and the Democratic Party made sweeping gains electing a President and a Democratic Congress. In 2010 the pendulum swung to the right and the Republicans made substantial gains including regaining the House of Representatives. The real question now is just where the pendulum lies. Can it go further to the right or will it begin to swing back to the left?

Currently we are experiencing a terrible gridlock over the budget problems. The debate revolves around whether to raise the debt limit, raise taxes or reduce spending. Neither the Democrats nor the Republicans will budge thus creating a huge and damaging stalemate. If we could put politics aside and simply come up with the right solution it would have to be to reduce spending and balance the budget. Raising taxes and increasing the debt limit will only compound the problem. The debate over the Country's budget problems is further complicated by the fact that the Country is still in the late stages of a recession that was begun in 2008. Unemployment is at a high level and the economy is stagnant.

To repeat what I have previously said the only way to get the economy moving ahead and to reduce unemployment is to put adequate purchasing power into the hands of every American because it is spending that will create a strong economy. And as I have indicated we must find a way to reduce labor costs and there must be a drastic reduction in income tax rates. I have proposed exempting the first $100,000 of income from taxes and taxing incomes above $100,000 at a maximum rate of 20%. This would release hundreds of billions of dollars into the economy and the increased economic activity would probably provide the government with greatly increased tax revenue.

It does not seem to make any difference whether the Democrats or the Republicans are in power although their ideological philosophies differ greatly. Under both parties government has continued to grow and the problems have become increasingly complex and severe. While the two party system is designed to allow one party to check the actions of the other this often results in a stalemate with little being accomplished. But it can also serve the Country well as was shown recently when the Tea Party faction of the Republican Party was able to block the attempt of the liberal Democrats to raise taxes at a time when raising taxes would have had a further devastating effect on the economy.

Right now in 2011 the Country is facing more serious problems than at any time that I can remember and that goes back a number of years. Neither the President nor the Congress seem able to take any constructive steps to solve these problems and they seem more interested in engaging in politics than they are in doing what is best for the Country. It is sort of a case where Washington fiddles while the United States burns. If the proper solutions are not found the Country will just drive off the cliff so to speak. This is difficult to understand because these are all decent and highly intelligent individuals who have a responsibility to the people who elected them to do what is best for the Country and they must know the consequences of their actions. But we have to remember that in another 20 years or so most of these people will no longer be around to see how their conduct today will affect the Country in the future. We need people who can put politics aside and just do the things that need to be done to put the Country on the right course that will create prosperity for every American.

Every so often I meet a young person who in my opinion is an outstanding individual. I am certain that there are millions more. This raises my hope that we do indeed have a new generation that will be more than capable of handling the Country's affairs in the future. The least we can do is to turn the Country over to them on a level playing field. We cannot leave them an insurmountable mountain which they will be unable to climb. The last thing we should want is to have future generations of Americans look back and point to the people who were running the Country in 2011 as those responsible for the Country's demise.

One of the most negative aspects of our political system is that we allow people to serve term after term almost making their election to public office a lifetime occupation. This is wrong and needs to be changed. For every public office the rule should be no more than two terms in office. It is absolutely essential that we have a turnover of people whereby we continuously bring in new faces with fresh ideas

I have often debated in my mind whether there should be a mandatory retirement age that would apply to people in public office but I am ruling that idea out. I will be 80 years old within a few months and while my health may not be 100% perfect it is good enough so that I could serve the American people for four years or eight years if that was their desire. There are people who are old at 70 and there are people who are young at 90. It all depends on the individual and I would never suggest that someone who is more than capable of performing their job be forced to retire just because they reach a certain age. And while I know that our Country generally tends to favor youth let us not forget that it is the oldest generation that has the wisdom and experience that the younger generations have yet to acquire.

A major problem with our political system is that it tends to work from the extremes of the political spectrum toward the middle instead of starting at the middle and working out to the extremes. In other words it is the extremes both left and right that attempt to control the political process. I would like to redefine the political spectrum by drawing a line that represents 100%. If we place a mark right at the middle it will be at the 50% point. This is where we need to start and I suggest that we go about 35% to the left and 35% to the right which will then give us 70% of the line. It is this broad center portion that represents Mr. and Mrs. Average American and the mainstream of our American society. The 15% at each end represent the extremes. We cannot allow these extremes on either end to be the tail that wags the political dog and most importantly we need the moderate politicians in the center to stand up and be accounted for and to take the leadership in shaping policies.

If it were up to me I would like to see a large national coalition built up around this 70%. It would include moderate democrats, moderate republicans, independents, Blacks, Hispanics, Asians and Whites. It would welcome all races, religions and nationalities. It would particularly welcome the 45 million senior citizens. And I would enlist input from labor unions in attempting to find fair and reasonable solutions to problems that affect all American workers. This would be an all American coalition built up around the center of the political spectrum. It would have some liberal views particularly on social issues and it would have some conservative views particularly regarding fiscal matters but it would not go to extremes. Politics and special interests would not become an influencing factor and the will of a majority of the people would govern. I would also change the names of the political parties calling the liberal Democrats the Liberal Party and the Tea Party and ultra conservative Republicans the Conservative party. Borrowing a name from World War I fame I would call this coalition party the Rainbow Party and I hope that all those who joint it will work together in a harmonious non-political manner. Every American should feel a sense of self-importance that they are somebody and that they are as equal to and no better or no worse than anyone else. By all working together the Rainbow Party can move our Country right down the center of the road and America will be better off for it.

TOPIC IX

THE FUTURE

If we had a crystal ball and could look out to the year 2050 and see what the demographics of the United States look like we would see a country far different than anything we have known. We would see a population of at least 400 million I am actually estimating something around 440 million. Broken down by race the population mix would look something like this: White 46%; Hispanic 30%; Black 16% and Asian and other non-white races 8%. This compares with the approximate current breakdown of White 66%; Hispanic 16%; Black 13% and Asian and other non-white races 5%. By the year 2050 the Hispanic and Black populations will be equal to the White population and if the Asian population is factored in the White population will be for the first time less than 50% of the total population.

To look out to the year 2100 becomes more difficult if not impossible as there are so many variables many of which cannot even be foreseen at this time. The population of the United States from 1900 to 2000 grew from around 100 million to approximately 300 million. If the population during the next hundred years grows at the same rate it would be around 900 million in 2100. This is probably very unrealistic and since no one alive today will be around to say I was wrong I am going to predict a population of 600 million for the year 2100. Of this total 38% will be Hispanic, 32% will be White, 20% Black and 10% Asian and other non-white races. Thus by the year 2100 the Hispanic and Black populations will outnumber the White population by an almost 2 to 1 ratio. I also predict that Spanish will have become the principal language in the United States replacing English which will remain a recognized language in much the same way that French is recognized in parts of Canada.

Looking beyond the year 2100 is impossible but it is probably safe to assume that the non-white population will continue to increase and the White population will become an increasingly more insignificant portion of the total population as time goes on. By 2100 the Hispanic and Black populations will probably have assumed total domination and control of the Country. No one can predict the effect on the White population when the United States becomes in effect an Hispanic and Black nation and the White population represents only an insignificant portion of the total population. It is entirely possible that sometime around the middle of the 22nd century when the White population gets down to 10% or 15% of the total population that there could very well be an exodus of the remaining White population out of the United States and into Canada. No one knows what the world will be like in the middle of the 22nd century but in looking at the globe the two least densely populated areas of the earth will probably be parts of Canada and parts of Siberia.

Attempting to predict population numbers for the year 2100 with any degree of accuracy is complicated because there are just too many unknown factors thus putting these predictions more in the category of a wild guess than anything else. To say that the population of the United States will increase from 300 million to 600 million or that the world population will increase from seven billion to 14 billion is based on projections of reasonable growth rates. There is no way of knowing if the resources of the earth will even be able to support this number of people or what the impact of floods, earthquakes, hurricanes, tornados, disease, famine or wars might have. The over crowding in some countries may force them to resort to drastic measures in order to either find living space and sufficient food for their population or else to find a way to thin out the population. In order to avoid these drastic measures it is probably not too soon for the United States and other nations around the world to begin to look ahead to the end of the 21st Century and give some thought as to how a doubling of the population can be handled. Perhaps by the early part of the 22nd century we will have found a way to establish colonies on the moon or on some planet in outer space.

I have seen various projections of population from different sources for both the United States and the world going out 50 and 100 years and beyond. The fact is they vary all over the lot and none of them can be relied upon as being entirely accurate. Some of these projections even predict a leveling off and then a decline in the total population which I find unrealistic and difficult to accept. The high and low estimates cover such a wide range that I feel that my estimates are no better or worse than any of the others. Of course it is entirely possible that the world population will continue to increase until such time as the resources of the earth can no longer support it at which time it will of necessity level off and begin to decline.

It is no secret that there is a great difference between the English speaking countries and the Spanish speaking countries as far as political stability, poverty levels and standard of living are concerned. Just compare the United States, Great Britain, Canada, Australia and New Zealand with the Latin American countries. Add to this the impact of the global economy which will over time lower the standard of living in all countries with high labor costs as wages must come down to a common denominator level. People my age will not be around in 20 or 30 years to see the changes that will have taken place nor will they be affected by them. But for someone born in the year 2011 they will be around to see the beginning of the 22nd century and are going to have to adjust to some very significant changes that their parents and grandparents would never have contemplated as being possible. It would do well for us to attempt now to plan for the future in a manner that will create the most favorable opportunities and living conditions for future generations of Americans.

I think we can take for granted that by the middle of the 21st Century the United States will have become a one party political system probably socialistic. I hope this does not happen but I am afraid that the direction the Country is taking and the future demographics of the population make this inevitable. This unfortunately is contrary to my own personal view that socialism would be bad for the Country but it will take a strong government to handle the sizeable population that will exist. We can only hope that the Country does not turn Fascist or Communist. The Hispanic and Black populations are the bastion of the Democratic Party and their shear numbers will greatly reduce the influence of the Republican Party. This is why the 2012 Presidential Election is so important for the Republican Party and why it must win the election. The Republican Party might do well if it spent a little less time having its candidates debating the issues among themselves and a little more time trying to cultivate the Hispanic and Black vote. It is entirely possible that the 2012 Presidential Election could be decided more by the demographics of the population and the personalities of the candidates rather than on the issues themselves. If the Republican Party is unable to capture the White House in 2012 the chances of winning it in future elections will become increasingly difficult if not impossible.

As I quoted at the beginning of this book from John Gunther's "Inside USA" socialism can lead directly to fascism and one can only wonder what this may mean for the American people in future years. The most pessimistic outlook for the Country by the middle of the 21st century would have unemployment being a huge problem far more serious than anything we are experiencing today as there will not be enough jobs to match the increase in population. Taxes will have been raised to levels that border on being confiscatory largely wiping out most personal savings. The people will be at the mercy of the government and the elite class will become those with the strongest political connections. The government will decide everything from where people live, to where they go to school to where they work how much they eat when they retire and whether or not they will receive health care benefits. The standard of living for everyone except for the political elite will be brought down to the lowest common denominator. And the benefits from programs such as Medicare and Social Security will have been so drastically reduced they will have a totally adverse effect on the older population. Anyone nearing the end of their life today should be thankful that they will not be around to live under these conditions.

One group that will suffer the most will be the senior citizens. There are currently approximately 45 million people in the United States over age 65 about 15% of the total population. If we assume that the government pays out an average of $15,000 a year in social security benefits, $15,000 in Medicare benefits and another $15,000 in miscellaneous benefits the government is spending an average of $45,000 a year on each senior citizen. Multiply this by the 45 million senior citizens and it amounts to approximately two trillion dollars a year being spent on everyone over age 65 and this does not include the people who will be turning 65 in future years. If we further assume the average age of these people is 75 years with a life expectancy of another 10 years this means the government will spend 20 trillion dollars until the last of these people have died. Now 20 trillion dollars is a lot of money. Of course a substantial portion of this money belongs to the senior citizens who contributed it through their payroll deductions and these funds are supposed to be kept in a separate trust fund but as long as the Federal Government borrows these funds and uses them for other than their intended purpose if we are not careful it is almost gives the impression that these funds belong to government rather than belonging to the social security beneficiaries.

It seems that in recent years the legislation has been going against the senior citizens. It is interesting that when the first draft of the healthcare legislation was released it contained the highly controversial provision that would have funded end of life conferences for senior citizens. Apparently someone decided that there would be unlimited Medicare funds available for any senior citizen who wanted to discuss end of life options with their doctor but when the healthcare legislation was finally passed it cut 500 billion dollars of Medicare benefits which might otherwise keep some senior citizens alive. If we also consider the cuts in nursing home reimbursements and the two year freeze on social security payments the senior citizens would have to question whether government has their best interests in mind. There is now talk about a proposed increase in the Medicare Part B premium for 2012 and it is hoped that there will be a cost of living increase that would prevent the senior citizens from seeing an actual reduction in the amount of their social checks. It should also be noted that the healthcare legislation that was passed is to some extent simply a redistribution of healthcare benefits which is evidenced by the reduction in Medicare benefits and the increased funding for Medicaid. The senior citizens need to become more aware of what is happening to them. After all, 45 million senior citizens can represent a formidable voting bloc.

We have no idea what life in the United States will be like by the year 2100 or even by 2050. Place yourself back in the year 1900 and try to look ahead 100 years and see how much the Country changed. Who in 1900 could have envisioned two world wars and numerous other wars. Who could have foreseen the automobile, the airplane, movies, radio, television, computers, cell phones, the internet, advances in medicine that have lengthened the human lifespan, China replacing the United States as the world's industrial leader and all the other changes that have taken place. And no one should forget the terrible reign of Nazi Germany which although it seemed an eternity only lasted 12 years or just 12% of the years of the century. If all of this happened in the hundred years from 1900 to 2000 who knows what will happen between now and the year 2100. We have 89 years to go and a lot can happen that we cannot even imagine at this time.

If there is one central message that I have tried to emphasize it is that the most serious problems that will have to be faced are all related to the tremendous increase in our population. These include creating enough jobs, finding ways to educate the population, finding enough food and living space, finding out how to handle another 100 million automobiles on our highways and even how to mesh the various components of this population into a harmonious and productive society. The solutions to these problems are not going to be easy and it must be remembered that we are now living in a world where everything that happens in any country around the world can affect the United States. If the president of Timbuktu sneezes it can have world wide repercussions. All one has to do is to look at the small country of Greece and its serious financial difficulties resulting from their overspending year after year and the devastating impact this is having on the United States and its citizens who are seeing their life savings negatively impacted as the stock market reacts to what is going on.

One of the things that will be very interesting to watch is the trend of prices. Just go back and compare the prices of things in 1900 with those in 1950 and then from 1950 to today. Prices of everything from restaurants, baseball games, rents, medical costs and college tuition have risen to astronomical levels. I remember in the late 1940s going to several baseball games at Yankee Stadium in New York City. It cost $1.25 for general admission, $2.00 for a box seat and you could get into the bleachers for 60 cents. A family of four going today can plan on spending several hundred dollars. When I was first married in 1960 our weekly food budget was $20.00 and for lunch I would spend around 35 cents. Our three and a half room apartment rent was $120 a month. Undoubtedly a major cause of the high prices today is the continuously decreasing value of the dollar. But I don't know how people can afford today's high prices and how long the trend to higher and higher prices can go on year after year. I recall in 1950 when my father died he was making $5,000 a year an average salary in those days and one that provided a reasonably comfortable standard of living. If you made $7,000 or $8,000 a year you were very well off and if you made $10,000 or more you were considered wealthy. My first job paid me $26.75 a week. Is the person making $50,000 a year in 2011 better off than the person who made $5,000 a year in 1950? I have my doubts about that. Will the average salary in 2050 be $500,000? At one time we talked about millions and billions of dollars. Now it is trillions of dollars. Where do we go from here? I remember when going to school during World War II hearing people joke about the German housewives going to the market with wheelbarrows full of money just to buy a loaf of bread. Don't laugh. The way our Country is going it could happen here. Perhaps by the year 2050 the Country's financial situation will have deteriorated to the extent that money will no longer have any value and everyone will be living in a planned government controlled society and dependent on government handouts.

I have painted a rather bleak picture for the future because serious questions are raised about whether we will have sufficient resources to support the tremendous increase in population that we will experience. What it comes down to is that unless a solution can be found there will be fewer resources to support an increased population. I don't know any other way to put this other than to say that it will mean a reduction in the standard of living for everyone. Job creation cannot keep up with our current population. Just how are we going to handle a population of 400, 500 or 600 million? Programs such as Medicare and Social Security are forecast to run out of funds in the not too distance future. Where will the funds come from to support these programs when the population is far greater than it is now? Will we be able to keep our two party political system and preserve democracy or will the Country fall to fascism? Will some terrorist organization get a hold of nuclear weapons and attempt to destroy the world? Can we provide a decent standard of living for every American or will the gap between the wealthy and the poor widen even further? This is very important because if this gap is allowed to widen it will set the stage for the kind of uprisings that are so prevalent in countries around the world today particularly in Europe and the Middle East. I suppose that if someone were to look at Thomas Cole's series of paintings "The Course of Empire" they might conclude that we are now in the third painting of the series "The Consummation of Empire." It remains to be seen if or when we go to the next painting in the series "The Destruction of Empire" to be followed by "The Ruins of Empire."

While we may think that we have serious problems today that must be dealt with these problems may turn out to be insignificant compared with the problems that will have to be dealt with in the future. While we may have a bright young generation that will be more than qualified to take over the Country's affairs their creative ability to solve these future problems will be taxed to the limit.

Regardless of what the population mix is or what kind of government will be in place a hundred years from now I do not think that anyone needs to worry about the United States losing its position as a powerful world leader. We do not have to take a back seat to anyone. Whatever problems that will exist in the United States are going to be far more severe in other nations around the world. Our values and traditions will survive even under the most adverse conditions. The thing about the American people has always been that even though in many respects we are a divided nation the people have always united in the face of any adversity and we have always overcome. While the United States in 50 or 100 years will have taken on a completely different character that would make a lot of people today very unhappy I predict that our Country will always remain the bastion of freedom and human rights and that we will always serve as a beacon of hope and inspiration for the rest of the world to admire.

It was Justice Oliver Wendell Holmes who talked about that little finishing canter just before dying. That final spurt of activity before one's life ends. While I hope to be around for many more years you never know and perhaps this book is my finishing canter. I hope it will serve a useful purpose or at least cause people to think more about the Country they are living in and where it is headed. There are many major issues and potential problems that will require satisfactory solutions.

In closing I would like to mention a short article that recently appeared in my local newspaper and which touched me greatly. It pertained to a buckskin quarter horse mare that had recently received an award for the best horse in the world in its class. The horse is owned by a women who lives in my hometown and was bred by her husband who unfortunately passed away and never lived to see his horse receive the award. When someone asked the horse's trainer if he thought the husband would be disappointed at not seeing his horse get the award the trainer responded by saying "no he had the best seat in the house." I can only hope that we will all be that fortunate.

We are living in an ever changing world and the future is very uncertain. It cannot be predicted. All we can do is to follow Longfellow's advice and wisely improve the present and go forth to meet the shadowy future without fear and with a manly heart.

Thank you for reading this and God Bless everyone.

www.ingramcontent.com/pod-product-compliance
Lightning Source LLC
Chambersburg PA
CBHW031257280526
45784CB00004B/1887